Records
Management

DEBBIE WEST, CPS

EMCParadigm

Developmental Editor	Michael Sander
Editorial Consultant	Susan Buie
Special Projects Coordinator	Joan D'Onofrio
Cover and Text Designer	Leslie Anderson
Illustrator	Colin Hayes
Desktop Specialist	Leslie Anderson
Proofreader	Joy McComb
Indexer	Nancy Fulton

Publishing Team: George Provol, Publisher; Janice Johnson, Director of Product Development; Lori Landwer, Marketing Manager; Shelley Clubb, Electronic Design and Production Manager

Library of Congress Cataloging in Publication Data

West, Debbie

Records management / Debbie West.

p. cm.

Includes index.

ISBN 0-7638-1428-8

1. Business records—Management. 2. Records—Management. 3. Filing systems.

HF5736 . W47 2001

651.5—dc21   200123732

Care has been taken to verify the accuracy of information presented in this book. The author, editor, and publisher, however, cannot accept any responsibility for Web, e-mail, newsgroup, or chat room subject matter or content, or for consequences from the application of information in this book, and make no warranty, expressed or implied, with respect to its content.

Trademarks: Some of the product names and company names included in this book have been used for identification purposes only and may be trademarks or registered trademarks of their respective manufacturers and sellers. The author, editor, and publisher disclaim any affiliation, association, or connection with, or sponsorship or endorsement by, such owners.

Text: ISBN 0-7638-1428-8   Order Number: 04533

Text Package: ISBN 0-7638-1328-1   Order Number: 01533

Photo Credits: Cover: M. Tcherevkoff/Image Bank; p. 4: David Raymer/The Stock Market; p. 5: CORBIS; p. 8: Andy Washnik/The Stock Market; p. 21: SuperStock; p. 24: SuperStock; p. 27: Courtesy of IBM and Verbatim Corporation; p. 43: Jon Feingersh/The Stock Market; p. 74: SuperStock; p. 79: JonFeingersh/The Stock Market.

© 2002 by Paradigm Publishing Inc.

Published by **EMC**Paradigm

875 Montreal Way

St. Paul, MN 55102

(800) 535-6865

E-mail: educate@emcp.com

Web Site: www.emcp.com

Printed in the United States of America

10 9 8 7 6 5 4 3 2

Contents

Preface   vi

Chapter 1

Records Management: The Big Picture   1
Even Cavemen Kept Records   2
Too Much Information!   3
Making a Federal Case of Records
    Management   5
What's What in Records Management   7
Records Management as a Career   8
Records Management in the Real World   12
Key Points   13
Memory File   14
Terms to Know   16
Make a Connection   16
Online Investigations   17
Thinking It Through   18

Chapter 2

Records Management Systems   19
Placing a Value on Records   20
Just How Important Is It?   21
How to Classify: What Is It For?
    Where Is It Going?   22
The Life Cycle of a Record   23
Records Storage Systems   24
Manual, Electronic, and Micrographic
    Records Systems   26
Integrating Records Systems   30
Records Management in the Real World   32
Key Points   34
Memory File   35
Terms to Know   38
Make a Connection   38
Online Investigations   39
Thinking It Through 40

Chapter 3

Evaluating Manual Records Systems   41
Assessing the Status Quo: Is the System
    Working? Can It Be Improved?   42
Retention Schedules: The Blueprint for
    Keeping or Tossing Records   44
Keeping Track with a Records
    Inventory   46
Records on the Move   48
Maintaining Control of Important
    Records   49
Keeping the Number of Forms Under
    Control   50
Records Management in the Real World   52
Key Points   54
Memory File   55
Terms to Know   58
Make a Connection   58
Online Investigations   59
Thinking It Through   60

Chapter 4

Manual Filing Systems   61
The Range of Manual Filing
    Arrangements   42
Alphabetic Card Records   72
How to Store Records   74
Requests and Chargeout Procedures for
    Records   78
Records Management in the Real World   82
Key Points   84
Memory File   85
Terms to Know   88
Make a Connection   88
Online Investigations   89
Thinking It Through   90

Chapter 5

Storage Solutions for Manual Records
    Systems   91
  Equipment   92
  Tools for Manual Filing Systems   96
  Nonstandard Equipment   102
  *Records Management in the Real
    World*   106
  Key Points   107
  Memory File   108
  Terms to Know   110
  Make a Connection   110
  Online Investigations   111
  Thinking It Through   112

Chapter 6

Classifying Records for a Manual
    System   113
  Personal or Individual Names   114
  Business or Company Names   118
  Other Names   123
  Storage by Subject within Alphabetic
    Arrangement   129
  Records Management in the Real World   130
  Key Points   131
  Memory File   132
  Terms to Know   134
  Make a Connection   134
  Online Investigations   139
  Thinking It Through   140

Chapter 7

Subject and Geographic Filing
    Arrangements   141
  Subject Filing   142
  Steps for Processing Records for Subject
    Filing   141
  Equipment and Supplies   144
  Indexes   145

Types of Subject Storage
    Arrangements   146
  Advantages of Subject Filing: Ease and
    Expandability   148
  Disadvantages of Subject Filing:
    Time and Money   149
  Geographic Filing   149
  Steps for Processing Records for
    Geographic Filing   151
  Equipment and Supplies   151
  Index   152
  Advantage of Geographic Filing:
    Easy Retrieval   153
  Disadvantage of Geographic Filing:
    Challenging to Learn   153
  Records Management in the Real World   154
  Key Points   155
  Memory File   156
  Terms to Know   158
  Make a Connection   158
  Online Investigations   161
  Thinking It Through   162

Chapter 8

Numeric Filing Arrangements   163
  Types of Numeric Filing
    Arrangements   164
  Chargeout Procedures   175
  Equipment and Supplies   176
  Alphabetic Index with Numeric
    Filing   177
  Records Management in the Real World   178
  Key Points   179
  Memory File   180
  Terms to Know   182
  Make a Connection   182
  Online Investigations   183
  Thinking It Through   184

Chapter 9

Micrographic Filing Systems   185

What Is Micrographics?   186
The History of Micrographics   187
Types of Microforms   187
Photographic Equipment   193
Retrieval and Viewing Equipment   193
Storage Equipment and Supplies   195
Reducing a Document to Film   196
Indexing and Coding during Filming   196
Processing or Developing the Film   197
Duplicating the Film   197
Merging Micrographics with Computer
   Technology   198
Cost Effectiveness of Micrographics   198
Legality of Micrographics   199
Records Management in the Real World   200
Key Points   201
Memory File   202
Terms to Know   204
Make a Connection   204
Online Investigations   205
Thinking It Through   206

Chapter 10

Computer-Based Records Systems   207

Computer-Based Records Systems   208
Organization of Databases   209

Database Management   211
How the Database and Computer
   Communicate   212
Records Storage in Computer-Based
   Systems   213
Data Security   214
Using E-Mail   215
Electronic Document Management
   Systems   219
Equipment and Process for Optical Disk
   Storage   219
Evaluation of Electronic Systems   222
Legality of Electronic Systems   222
Records Management in the Real World   224
Key Points   226
Memory File   227
Terms to Know   230
Make a Connection   230
Online Investigations   231
Thinking It Through   232

Glossary   233

Answers to Memory File Questions   240

Index   243

Preface

Records Management teaches a practical, hands-on approach to all types and complexities of filing systems in a user-friendly, conversational manner. This textbook provides a human dimension to the study of records management with interviews and lively case studies. In the textbook's ten chapters, the student will become proficient in the key filing systems, including manual, subject, geographic, numeric, micrographic, and electronic. Interactive exercises throughout the textbook will assess the student's understanding of the principles and concepts supporting each system.

ONLINE INVESTIGATIONS. Each chapter of the textbook has a section of projects to be researched online. (This section may be optional, depending on the availability of equipment.) These projects allow the student to have hands-on experience in completing in-depth research on the Internet.

PRACTICE KIT. New Media Publishing is a multifaceted organization with various locations, including a printing plant and bookstores. The Practice Kit contains 180 filing documents for the student to read and file in alphabetic, subject, chronological, and numeric filing arrangements, with cross-references in several situations. The Practice Kit is an authentic simulation of the filing practices used in contemporary business and industry. The documents are of standard 8 ½ x 11" size, filed into an accordion folder for a "student friendly" package.

DATA DISK. The data disk contains four projects to be completed by the student in Microsoft® Excel, Access, and Word, and Windows Explorer. The numeric portion in Microsoft Excel may be keyed prior to filing in the practice kit. The database project will teach the student how to key, add, delete, and perform a query. The student will learn how to create folders and move documents from one medium to another in Windows Explorer, as well as how to move information from one file to another in Microsoft Word.

INSTRUCTOR'S GUIDE. The Instructor's Guide provides suggested activities and teaching aids, including crossword puzzles and word games, to accompany the chapters in the textbook. Answers to the "Make a Connection" and "Thinking It Through" questions and the filing applications in Chapter 6 are included. Midterm and final examinations are in the Instructor's Guide. The 20 numeric filing projects are printed in the Instructor's Guide for instructors who do not wish to have the students key this project on the data disk.

ACKNOWLEDGMENTS. I would like to thank all of the individuals who graciously granted interviews for this textbook, and the business owners for access to their organizations and employees. In particular, I could not have completed this textbook without the support and encouragement of my students, co-workers, friends, and family, as well as my publishing company.

Debbie West, CPS

Records Management: The Big Picture

1

Why Records Management Matters to Business, Government, and You

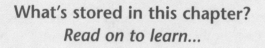

What's stored in this chapter?
Read on to learn...

📁 Why it is important to keep accurate records in business and in our personal lives

📁 The history of recorded information

📁 Legislation affecting how information is handled

📁 How the Information Age has influenced records management procedures

📁 The language of records management

📁 Careers in records management

All businesses need information. To survive in the marketplace, businesses need to have systems in place to manage the information vital to their work. To help a business run smoothly, these systems must be designed to permit the correct storage and rapid retrieval of information. Everything from invoices to letters to legal contracts and much, much more must be stored in a logical, efficient way.

Questions?

Why is records management so important in the workplace?

Why is records management so important in the workplace? The short answer is that it is a financial issue. A business that manages its records inefficiently will waste time (and money) searching for information. Legal reasons also motivate businesses to manage their information appropriately. For example, both individuals and businesses are required to maintain tax records for at least three years or risk penalties from the Internal Revenue Service. Did you really need reminding?

So, yes, records management IS important. Which means individuals responsible for managing and maintaining records systems are key contributors to business. If you are responsible for records management in your work, you can have a positive and rewarding impact on your company's success.

Even Cavemen Kept Records

As amazing as it may seem, record-keeping activities can be traced back to cave dwellers. Think of the prehistoric drawings

Figure 1-1 Prehistoric cave drawings are an early example of record keeping.

discovered on cave walls around the world (see Figure 1-1). Using clay writing instruments and a palette of rock, our predecessors recorded important events. Moving along in history, people graduated to clay tablets and parchments to document their lives. By the late 1800s, the first filing systems were developed, quickly evolving into the wooden vertical filing cabinets that debuted in the early 1900s.

As office equipment developed in the early 1900s, more **documents** (official business records) were being retained by offices, and systematic record keeping became essential. By 1914, alphabetical filing had been adopted as a records management strategy in large businesses. At the same time, business and secretarial schools began to routinely teach filing techniques.

Billions of paper documents containing vital information pass through the hands of office workers every year. Yet many organizations do not understand the importance of retaining knowledgeable, trained records personnel. Instead, the need for staff dedicated to records management goes unnoticed until the problem—disorganized documentation—disrupts some aspect of the business.

Putting records management systems in place ex post facto (after the fact) is an expensive and time-consuming proposition, but it can be done. For optimal operational efficiency, a business should assign to at least one person the task of managing and standardizing procedures for the handling of documents, and periodically review the effectiveness of the systems in place.

Questions?

When should trained records personnel be put into place?

Too Much Information!

We are living in the **Information Age**, an era characterized by increased access to and reliance on information in its many forms. This evolution to an **Information Society** has been made possible by rapidly evolving technology. Advances in technology have contributed tools that help people produce, reproduce, and distribute information. These tools (the personal computer, for example) have become more common and more affordable, bringing information on demand to nearly all levels of society.

There has never been a time when more people had more access to information, on a global basis, than right now.

Technology in the Information Age has changed how organizations operate, helping to increase workplace **productivity**. Why are businesses able to accomplish more? A wide array of technologies speed up business processes and make them more efficient, meaning more work gets done. Here is an example of how things happen more quickly in today's workplace. Suppose you have an important document to deliver to a customer in a foreign nation. A few years back, the sole option for delivering the document (without having to get on a plane to hand-deliver it) would have been to send it by postal mail. You might have chosen to pay a premium for faster delivery. Now you can send the document electronically, using a fax machine or electronic mail

(e-mail). Using either method, the document arrives at its destination within a few seconds or minutes, instead of taking days to arrive by postal service.

While technology has helped business move more quickly, it has not helped to reduce the amount of information businesses need to manage. What technological advances have done is increase capacity for and capabilities relating to information management. In the office environment, technology has affected all aspects of office procedures and functions, especially record storage.

Until word processing equipment came along, office personnel typed documents using manual or electric typewriters. If multiple copies were required, the typist layered onionskin paper with sheets of carbon copying paper. The task was made more cumbersome every time a mistake was made. To correct a typographical error, the typist had to physically erase each sheet of paper and then retype the letter or word. In contrast, today's office worker can easily key, edit, and duplicate copies of a document using standard tools of the business office: personal computer, printer, and photocopier.

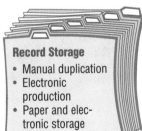

Record Storage
- Manual duplication
- Electronic production
- Paper and electronic storage

Despite the rise in electronic record-keeping practices, most of us like to be able to touch documents that are important to us.

The overall increase in paper records produced by businesses is directly related to the rise in electronic equipment such as the computer, printer, facsimile (fax) machine, and photocopier. A new category of records—electronic files—must also be properly stored.

Making a Federal Case of Records Management

In the United States, records management is more than a business concern. The U.S. government has demonstrated a keen interest in how information is handled, to protect its own interests as well as those of its citizens.

In 1946 President Harry Truman realized the necessity of systematic records management and established the **Hoover Commission** to study the needs of record keeping by government agencies. This committee recommended that legislation be established requiring adequate records management programs in all departments of the federal government. In 1949 the **Federal Property and Administration Services Act** created the **General Services Administration (GSA)**, incorporating the **National Archives**. The Act authorized the GSA to conduct departmental records surveys to establish procedures for storing and retaining records.

1946	Hoover Commission
1949	General Services Administration (GSA)
1954	*Guide to Record Retention Requirements* published
1966	Freedom of Information Act
1968	National Archives and Records Administration (NARA)
1974	Privacy Act
1980	Paperwork Reduction Act
1982	Project ELF
1996	Electronic Freedom of Information Act

In 1954 a second Hoover Commission was established to set record retention schedules for all government departments. The first ***Guide to Record Retention Requirements*** was published as a result of the commission's findings. This guide is still being updated and published by the GSA.

In 1968 the GSA's responsibilities were assumed by the **National Archives and Records Administration (NARA)**, an independent federal agency that helps preserve the nation's history by overseeing the management of all federal records.

Two important legislative acts were passed in 1966 and 1974 regarding individual rights and records management. In 1966 the **Freedom of Information Act** granted individuals the right to request information from federal agencies, except records that are protected from disclosure to the extent that the exemptions are contained in the law or by one of the three special law-enforcement record exclusions. In 1974 the **Privacy Act** provided individuals with the ability to access information about themselves, the right to exclude others from obtaining information, and the right to know who has accessed their records. Just six years later, the **Paperwork Reduction Act** of 1980 was passed. This legislation addresses the need for better management of paperwork.

Professional organizations have influenced the legislative process in favor of better standards for records management. The **Association of Records Managers and Administrators (ARMA)** began **Project ELF** (Eliminate Legal-size Files). Their campaign was so successful that in 1983 the Judicial Conference of the United States voted to use only letter-size paper in all federal courts. By 1984 many state and local governments had begun to make the change from legal-size paper to letter-size paper.

The Freedom of Information Act was amended by the **Electronic Freedom of Information Act** of 1996. This amendment grants public access to government documents through the federal government's Electronic Reading Room on the Internet.

New records management legislation will continue to be passed throughout the twenty-first century. As technology grows and more information is created by either hard or soft copy documents, new methods and procedures must be established to control document overload and facilitate fast retrieval of information.

The Internet has raised new concerns about privacy of information.

Learn About Careers from ARMA

A great resource for individuals interested in a records management career is the **Association of Records Managers and Administrators (ARMA)**. ARMA is the leading professional organization of personnel in the records management and information fields, offering training and networking opportunities through its 150+ U.S. and international chapters. Monthly chapter meetings are held along with special workshops and conferences. Contact ARMA to learn more about the benefits of membership.

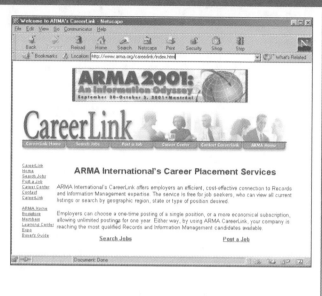

ARMA
4200 Somerset Drive, Suite 215
Prairie Village, KS 66208
E-mail: hg@arma.org
Web site: www.arma.org

What's What in Records Management

As with any area of specialization, records management has its own jargon. The following discussion and definitions of frequently used terms will help your understanding of the field:

Records management is the systematic control of all records, from their creation or receipt, through processing, distribution, application, storage, and retrieval, to their final disposition.

A **record** is recorded information pertinent to a business function. Records take several forms. The terms **hard copy** and **hard record** refer to a paper document that eventually may be transferred to electronic form. A **soft copy** is output seen on a computer screen or in microimages. While the term **file** refers to a collection of related records, it should not to be confused with the term **electronic file**, which describes a mode of storage by computer.

Questions?

What are some of the specialized terms of records management?

The **filing system** is the type of system used to store records; it describes the manner in which the records are organized. There are three types of record filing systems, which, for optimal efficiency (meaning fast access), should be integrated in organizations that use all three.

Manual records system. This is the system for physical storage and retrieval of hard copy records. Essentially, it refers to filing "by hand," the oldest method of records management (see Figure 1-2). Manual records systems are frequently enhanced by micrographic and electronic systems.

Micrographic records system. This type of system uses special photography to reduce hard copy records to microimages for space-saving storage. Micrographics reduce the bulk of records while still permitting rapid retrieval. This convenient method of storage is ideal for organizations required to maintain large volumes of records indefinitely, such as banks, newspapers, and insurance companies.

Electronic records system. This term refers to the storage and retrieval of records by computer. Electronic systems can store large volumes of information on floppy disks, optical disks, CD-ROMs, CD-RWs, and the hard drive of a computer.

Figure 1-2 Filing "by hand" is the oldest method of records management.

Records Management as a Career

There are many diverse career opportunities in the area of records management. Actual job responsibilities in the records management department of an organization will vary depending upon the systems the organization employs to store records.

Most organizations rely upon some form of records management for day-to-day operations.

In some organizations, a centralized **Records and Information Management (RIM) department** includes all manual, micrographic, and electronic storage systems as well as computer-related systems. A **records and information director or manager** oversees the systems and divisional managers or supervisors for each system. **Records clerks** work with each records supervisor to maintain the records center.

If the organization does not have a designated RIM department, each department's administrative staff oversees their own records. Most small organizations will use a decentralized records systems. Table 1-1 shows a sample organizational chart depicting the hierarchy of records management personnel in a typical business. The organizational chart shows the layout of a records center in an organization. The titles of personnel, the number of personnel, and the different departments will vary from one organization to another.

Questions?
What is the range of job opportunities in records management?

Table 1-1 Organizational chart displaying hierarchy of records management personnel.

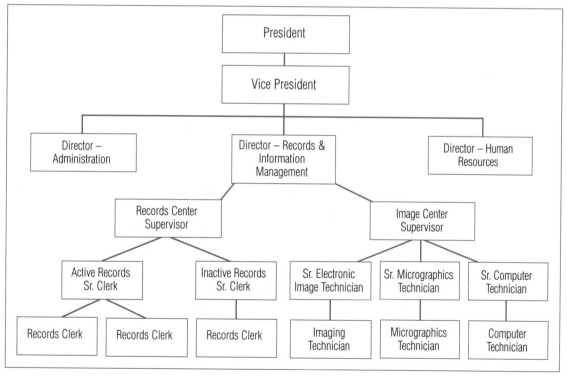

Get Certified as a Records Manager

The **Institute of Certified Records Managers (ICRM)** is an international certifying organization for professional records and information managers. It was started in 1975 so records and information personnel could be measured, accredited, and recognized according to criteria established by their peers. ICRM also serves as the official certifying organization for the Association of Records Managers and Administrators (ARMA).

The ICRM sponsors the **Certified Records Manager (CRM)** examination. The test, given twice a year, in May and November, consists of six parts. Parts 1 through 5 consist of 100 multiple-choice questions each; Part 6 requires written essay responses.

Part 1: Management principles and the records and information management program
Part 2: Records creation and use
Part 3: Records systems, storage, and retrieval
Part 4: Records appraisal, retention, protection, and disposition
Part 5: Facilities, supplies, and technology
Part 6: Case studies

Learn more about ICRM and the CRM examination on the Internet at www.icrm.org.

Archives and off-site storage centers employ **file clerks** to file and retrieve records for their customers. In this type of environment, the records manager oversees the general operation of the archive or off-site storage center and must be knowledgeable regarding all manual, micrographic, and electronic storage systems.

The sample job descriptions in Figures 1-3 and 1-4 provide a glimpse of requirements for working in the records management field. As you can see, people management skills are often just as important as records management skills, particularly as the level of supervisory responsibility increases.

Figure 1-3 Sample job description for a Senior Records Clerk, Active Records

Senior Records Clerk, Active Records The Senior Records Clerk is responsible for the daily activities of active records and reports to the Records Center Supervisor.
Position responsibilities: 1. Develop and maintain the work schedules for records staff 2. Assign and oversee job duties to records staff 3. Retrieve requested files and information 4. Maintain retention schedule of records 5. Oversee the transfer of records to inactive storage by the established retention schedule 6. Supervise and evaluate the records staff
Position requirements: 1. Ability to move and lift 20 pounds 2. Excellent written and oral communication skills 3. Excellent organizational and planning skills 4. Ability to work with peers and supervisory staff 5. Knowledge of computer technology 6. Ability to supervise employees
Education/experience: Two (2) years experience as a records clerk in a records center and/or a minimum of two (2) years college or an associate degree with coursework in records management, computer technology and management.

Figure 1-4 Sample job description for an Image Records Supervisor

Image Records Supervisor The Image Records Supervisor is responsible for the supervision of the Image Records of the organization and reports to the Director of Records and Information Management.
Position responsibilities: 1. Train and hire new employees in the Image Center 2. Develop and implement the procedures for records staff 3. Supervise all image records staff 4. Conduct performance evaluations of staff 5. Prepare departmental yearly budget 6. Oversee departmental costs and company allocation costs 7. Develop the retention schedule of image records
Position requirements: 1. Knowledge of image and computer technologies 2. Excellent written and oral communication skills 3. Excellent organizational and planning skills 4. Ability to supervise employees 5. Ability to plan and organize work 6. Critical thinking and problem-solving skills 7. Excellent decision-making skills 8. Ability to perform under pressure
Education/experience: A minimum of six (6) years experience in active or inactive records center or an image records center with increasing supervisory experience. A minimum of two (2) years education with emphasis in computer and information technology and records management with CRM certification.

Records Management in the Real World

The Specialty Clothing Store

Elite is a specialty clothing shop with two salespersons and one manager/owner. The shop's records are handled by one person, the store manager. This small business is able to manage all of its documentation using a manual filing system. The store manager uses a general alphabetical filing system to house all records pertaining to manufacturer, designer, and style of clothing. A numeric filing system is employed to manage all of the accounts payable and receivable. Records documenting earnings and expenses are kept for tax purposes, as required by law. The store manager maintains chronological files of merchandise order due dates and future market dates. Because the store's sales staff works on a commission basis, sale records and return merchandise are accurately logged to ensure that payroll checks are accurate. Compared to some businesses, the specialty clothing store maintains a relatively low volume of information. Because of the size of the organization, the company has not invested in a computerized system.

For better understanding, review and reflect on the key points of this chapter.

Businesses rely on information to operate efficiently. Records management is the systematic control of all records from their conception to their disposal.

Today is the Information Age. Changing technology has increased the speed with which we do business (our productivity) and the volume of information businesses must manage. Many technologies have enhanced and simplified methods for records management.

There are three types of record filing systems: manual, micrographic, and electronic. An organization may use one or more systems integrated to achieve an efficient records program. Trained personnel are a key factor to the success of any records system.

The U.S. government issues laws governing the proper management of business and personal records. These laws are designed to protect individual privacy, ensure access to information, and dictate the length of time certain records are maintained.

Records management is a growing field offering diverse career opportunities. The Institute of Certified Records Managers (ICRM) and the Association of Records Managers and Administrators (ARMA) are two organizations dedicated to the professional development of records management personnel.

True or False?
Rewrite each false item to make it a true statement.

1. The survival of all businesses depends upon having information available for use when it is needed.
2. The management of records in an organization is not vital to decision making or the organization's existence.
3. The keeping of records is relatively new and can only be traced back to the early 1900s.
4. With the amount of records being produced in business today, this era is called the Technology Age.
5. The use of paper documents is decreasing in businesses today.
6. Manual filing systems have been made obsolete by micrographic and electronic records systems.
7. President Truman established the first commission to study the needs of systematic record keeping.
8. The General Services Administration was created to develop procedures for storing and retaining government records.
9. Project ELF was a campaign by ARMA to eliminate legal-size files.
10. Legislation addressing the need for better managing paperwork was called the Paperwork Reduction Act of 1980.
11. A file is a group of related records.
12. There are very few career opportunities in the area of records management.
13. An organizational chart will show the layout of the records center of an organization.
14. The CRM examination is a six-part examination sponsored by the Institute of Certified Records Managers.
15. ARMA is the Association of Records Managers and Administrators and is the leading professional organization of the records management and information fields.

Multiple Choice
Choose the best answer from those provided.

1. The first records system began with: a) prehistoric drawings; b) clay tablets; c) the 1800s; d) the 1900s.
2. Official business records are called: a) papers; b) reports; c) documents; d) files.
3. The systematic control of records from creation to disposal is called: a) document management; b) records management; c) records organization; d) administrative document management.

4. With the use of technology, today has been called the: a) Technology Era; b) Internet Era; c) Electronic Age; d) Information Age.

5. The three types of records systems are: a) manual, micrographic, computer; b) paper, microforms, electronic; c) manual , micrographic, electronic; d) manual, electronic, Internet.

6. A collection of related records is called a/an: a) index; b) file; c) document; d) list.

7. The Hoover Commission was established to study record keeping in federal agencies by: a) President Hoover; b) President Roosevelt; c) President Truman; d) President Eisenhower.

8. The legislative act that granted individuals the right to request information from federal agencies, except records protected from disclosure by exemptions contained in the law or by one of the three special law-enforcement record exclusions, was: a) the Privacy Act; b) Project ELF; c) the Hoover Commission; d) the Freedom of Information Act.

9. In 1974, this legislation provided individuals with the ability to access information about themselves, the right to exclude others from obtaining information, and the right to know who has accessed their records. It is called: a) the Hoover Commission; b) Project ELF; c) the Privacy Act; d) the Freedom of Information Act.

10. Recorded information pertinent to a business function is called a: a) ledger; b) record; c) list; d) file.

11. A _____ describes how records are organized: a) records arrangement; b) records order; c) filing sequence; d) filing system.

12. Another term for a paper document is a: a) soft copy; b) hard copy; c) print copy; d) carbon copy.

13. The drawing showing the layout of the records center of an organization is called a/an: a) departmental chart; b) job description; c) organizational chart; d) organizational summary.

14. The six-part examination sponsored by the Institute of Certified Records Managers is called the: a) CRM examination; b) CPS examination; c) CRMA examination; d) CLA examination.

15. The acronym ARMA stands for the organization: a) Administrators of Records Management Association; b) Association of Records Managers and Administrators; c) Association of Records Managers and Associates; d) Associates of Records Managers and Administrators.

Terms to Know

Write definitions of these terms to increase your knowledge of the records management field.

disposition
document
electronic file
electronic records system
file
filing system
hard copy

hard record
manual records system
micrographic records system
record
records management
soft copy

Make a Connection

Write or discuss your response to each question.

1. What is the benefit of integrating manual, micrographic, and electronic records systems?

2. Why is it important for a business to assign responsibility for records management to one or more individuals? What types of problems can be avoided by establishing guidelines for records management?

3. Discuss two pieces of legislation governing the distribution and accessibility of information. What do these laws prevent? Do you think they are necessary?

4. Investigate the policies of a foreign nation regarding access to personal information. Compare the policy to U.S. legislation. Do you agree with the other country's policies? Defend your opinion.

5. Which responsibilities listed in the job descriptions in Figures 1-3 and 1-4 appeal to you? Which do you feel most prepared to handle? Are there any that concern you?

6. Of what value is certification by the Institute of Certified Records Managers (ICRM)? Why might employers prefer individuals with this credential?

The following activities require a computer and Internet connectivity.

1. Visit the following Web sites representing records management organizations. Describe the information offered. Rate the sites based on depth of information and ease of use (use a 10-point scale).

   - National Archives and Records Administration (NARA) www.nara.gov
   - Institute of Certified Records Managers (ICRM) www.icrm.org
   - Association of Records Managers and Administrators (ARMA) www.arma.org

2. Visit the following job boards on the Internet and search for positions requiring records management skills. Note that most of the job boards list records management positions within an administrative or clerical category. Print a job description that interests you.

   - www.emcp.net/monster
   - www.emcp.net/hotjobs
   - www.emcp.net/flipdog

Dig deeper to apply what you have learned.

1. In this chapter, we discussed why records are kept by organizations. Think about how you manage your personal records. How does accurate record keeping play a role in your daily life? In what ways are your own records organized or disorganized?

2. Review the records systems of the specialty clothing store discussed in this chapter. Make a case for conversion to an electronic records system.

3. Talk with a manager who works in records management for an organization, or someone who handles the records of a small firm. Explain to the class the company's records systems. After viewing the existing system of the organization, discuss any changes you would make if you were in charge of the company's records system.

Records Management Systems 2

How Records Are Identified and Stored

What's stored in this chapter?
Read on to learn...

- The different values of records
- How records are classified
- The life cycle of a record
- The features of manual, micrographic, and electronic records storage systems

Invoices. Bills of lading. Letters. Memos. Records take many forms and fulfill many purposes. One of the critical tasks of records management is to determine which records should be kept and which are of no long-term value.

When a record is determined to have value, it is placed in some form of records system for storage. Records systems vary, but they all are intended to maintain records in an organized, easy-to-access format.

Placing a Value on Records

Throughout your school years, you may have saved some of the work you produced in the classroom. Your personal archives may include an art project, the spelling tests you aced, and maybe a term paper or two. You probably also saved your report cards. From a personal perspective, the art project may hold more significance than any other aspect of your school work, giving it a greater perceived value. However, from a historical and legal perspective, your report cards have greater actual value because they document your attendance and performance.

As this example illustrates, the actual value of a record is based on its function. In business, records have four general categories of value: historical, operational, legal, and fiscal.

Historical records. Records of this nature have long-term value and tell the story of an organization. They may serve as a basis for future managerial decisions. These records are stored in the records archive and should be periodically reviewed for their historical value.

Operational records. These records provide necessary information about the daily operation of the organization. Examples include letters, memorandums, and reports. Operational records may have a long-term or short-term retention and

Que**stions**?
What determines the value of a record?

disposal schedule. The user should be consulted to determine the value and useful life span of a given operational record.

Legal records. Records of this type need to be maintained as required by law or for litigation purposes. Legal records include articles of incorporation, stockholder reports, meeting minutes, deeds of property or ownership, contracts, and other legal documents essential to operate an organization. The organization's legal counsel should be consulted when determining the appropriate retention and disposal schedules of records.

Records Categories
- Historical
- Operational
- Legal
- Fiscal

Fiscal records. These records have both operational and legal value. They include accounts receivable, accounts payable, financial reports, bank statements, cancelled checks, employee payroll records, and budgets. All organizations are required to keep fiscal records for a prescribed time period. In addition, all organizations, like individuals, are subject to evaluation by the Internal Revenue Service and must provide accurate financial and tax information. Failure to maintain accurate records could result in fines and penalties to the government. The fiscal officer or chief financial officer of the organization must approve the destruction of fiscal records.

Just How Important Is It?

Business records can also be categorized according to four levels of usefulness: vital, important, useful, and nonessential.

Vital records. As the name implies, these records are essential to the organization. They are critical to the legal, fiscal, historical, and operational functions of the organization. Vital records answer the who, how, where, and when questions about the organization.

Levels of Usefulness
- Vital
- Important
- Useful
- Nonessential

Important records. These records are necessary to the continuation of the organization. In case of destruction or loss, they can be reproduced at a great cost.

Useful records. These records are needed for the everyday operation of the organization, but they are not as critical to the legal, fiscal, or historical functions of a business. If lost or destroyed, the missing documents may cause delay or inconvenience, but probably will not ruin the business.

Nonessential records. Once they have served their purpose, these documents land in the circular file (the garbage can or recycling bin). An example of a nonessential record would be a memo announcing the company picnic. Once the picnic is over, there is no reason to keep the announcement.

How to Classify: What Is It For? Where Is It Going?

Records can be classified in two ways: by their use and by their destination (see Table 2-1). Records classified by use may be **reference documents** or **transaction documents**. You might think of this as a distinction between those documents that are used to gather information (reference) and those used to get something done (transaction). Records classified by destination include documents with an **internal audience** and those with an **external audience**.

Table 2-1 Classification of Documents by Use or Destination

CLASSIFICATIONS

How a Document Is Used	Where a Document Ends Up
Reference documents These documents explain how and why procedures are maintained by the organization, or they may contain information vital to the operation of the organization. Examples include historical documents and procedures manuals.	**Internal documents** These documents are used within a company and are not distributed outside the organization. Examples include personal correspondence, memos, and financial statements.
Transaction documents These documents are used to conduct the everyday operations of the organization. Examples include general correspondence, fiscal documents, legal documents, and daily operational documents.	**External documents** These documents are intended for an audience external to the organization. Examples include documents sent to individuals and companies doing business with the organization; documents sent to federal, state, and local agencies; and documents received from outside sources.

The Life Cycle of a Record

The life cycle of a record describes the stages a record goes through from the time it is "born" to the time it reaches its final "resting place" (see Figure 2-1). The following five stages describe the record life cycle:

Step 1: Creation. A record is created when data is recorded in a usable form. A business record typically might be an invoice, a letter, a completed form, or a legal document. It can be created manually or by a variety of means aided by technology.

Step 2: Distribution. This describes the stage at which a document is physically or electronically delivered to its intended audience. Typical forms of distribution include postal delivery, computer transmissions, courier services, and facsimile (fax) transmissions.

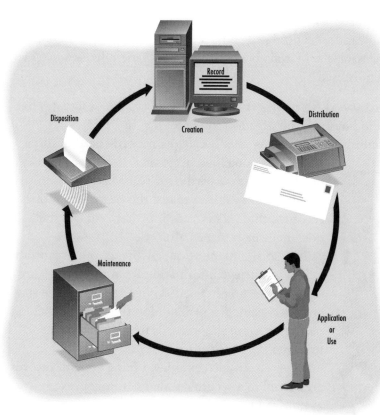

Figure 2-1 The Typical Life Cycle of a Record

Step 3: Application or use. This step describes the reason the record was created in the first place. Records are used to inform decisions, educate groups, and collect statistics, among other things.

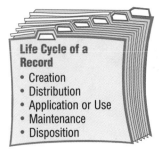

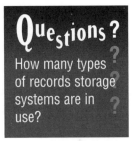

Life Cycle of a Record
- Creation
- Distribution
- Application or Use
- Maintenance
- Disposition

Step 4: Maintenance. Maintenance refers to the proper preservation of a record from its creation through its distribution and use. This step includes security, storage, and retrieval procedures for business records.

Step 5: Disposition. The last step in the life cycle describes what happens to the record once it has fulfilled its original purpose. If there is a legal or business requirement to maintain the information, a record may be transferred to archives (long-term storage). When records are no longer useful to the operation of the organization, they may be disposed of.

Records Storage Systems

There are two types of records storage systems used in organizations: centralized and decentralized. An organization's policies, size, and available personnel will generally dictate which system is used.

Que**s**t**ions?**

How many types of records storage systems are in use?

Centralized filing systems. This type of system designates one area to house all the organization's records. In a large organization, this area is usually called a **records center** and is staffed with qualified personnel. When employees need to retrieve a hard copy record stored in this type of system, they must request the record from the records center. The records center requires the document be returned after use.

In a small organization, anyone in the organization is free to retrieve information from the storage area, creating essentially a self-service set-up. Office staff are responsible for maintaining the records, including periodically purging records that have become nonessential over time.

In an electronic centralized filing system, records are stored in a secure **database**. Employees authorized to access the database use assigned security codes to log in from workstation computers.

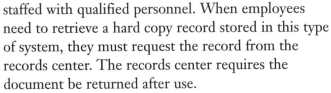

Security clearance to a centralized filing system will depend upon the user's need to access information. For example, executives and managers may have secure access to employee financial data that is restricted to the general employee population.

An advantage of the centralized filing system is that records are easily retrieved from one location. Trained personnel and proper control procedures are necessary to ensure that the records are properly maintained.

Decentralized filing systems. For some organizations, it makes better sense to house records in more than one location throughout the organization, creating a decentralized filing system. The junior college described at the end of this chapter is an excellent example of how a decentralized filing system operates. At the junior college, each department has its own records system and restricts access to the records to authorized personnel.

With an electronic decentralized filing system, individual users have their own files stored in the hard drives of their workstation computers. Access to a networked system may be available in large organizations.

The advantage of a decentralized filing system is that records are housed in the area that mainly uses those records, permitting tighter control of important documents. A disadvantage is that someone outside the immediate area may have more difficulty locating and retrieving a record from within the system.

Storage Systems
- Centralized
- Decentralized

Taking Charge of Records with a Chargeout Program

Organizations with either a centralized or a decentralized records system can benefit from a process that helps keep track of where records are at all times. A chargeout program requires employees to sign out records they need to use. The program also may specify a due-back date and ask what the record will be used for. Chargeout programs help establish accountability and also ensure responsible use of important records.

GLOBE-WEISS 9 OUT 1 ⊕ Minimum10% Post Consumer Recycled Content					OUT
TAKEN BY	NUMBER, SUBDIVISION OR NAME	DATE	TAKEN BY	NUMBER, SUBDIVISION OR NAME	
mc	Tara Fuller	01/06			
JC	Marci Carbonneau	01/06			
TF	Shawn Collins	04/09			
TF	Michelle Massey	01/07			
MM	Iruna Roberts	04/14			
TR	Keya te Carroll	04/19			
JX	Niko Johnson	1/20			
MC	Terrence te Young	1/20			
TR	Saturna Forst	02/01			
aW	Andi Dale	2/4			

Manual, Electronic, and Micrographic Records Systems

Most organizations use more than one type of system to manage their record storage needs. Nearly all organizations manually maintain some of their records. More and more organizations manage at least some of their records using micrographic and electronic means. In addition, very large organizations may rely on micrographic systems to manage the large volumes of records they generate.

Manual records systems. The most basic method for filing documents is to do so "by hand," organizing documents using an alphabetical filing arrangement. While it may seem overly simple, the manual system has many advantages, even in our electronic society. With a manual system, users can quickly locate hard copy records (assuming the volume of records is not excessive). Manual record keeping does not generally require special training, which saves costs over other methods.

There are a few drawbacks to the manual system. Large companies that produce great volumes of records will quickly be burdened by a manual system that takes up office space. In addition, the cost of supplies, equipment, and space can be significant. Also, manual records systems are prone to user error, meaning misfiled records. Since a manual system is less likely to be assigned qualified records personnel, it may also suffer from the lack of control procedures.

Manual record-keeping systems are perfectly suitable for small organizations like the specialty clothing shop described in Chapter 1. Most small organizations can maintain adequate control of their records because only a few people need access to the filing system.

Electronic records systems. Electronic records systems are more complex than manual systems because they require special equipment. Employees required to use the equipment will need training to perform records management tasks.

Q**uestions?**

Do organizations use more than one type of system to manage storage needs?

With an electronic system, records are stored using a computer and some type of media, such as hard disk, CD-ROM disks, CD-RW disks, floppy disks, optical disks, and magnetic tapes (see Figure 2-2). Electronic records systems include:

- **Database programs.** Database software allows the user to develop databases for storing information. A database can be customized to the organization's needs and permits fast retrieval of information through automated searches.

- **Word processing programs.** Word processing software permits the creation and storage of text files.

- **Spreadsheet programs.** Spreadsheet software helps to organize numbers and make calculations to determine payroll, budgets, inventory, and more.

Figure 2-2 Floppy diskette, hard disk, tape reel, and tape cartridge are all media used for electronic data storage.

An important benefit of electronic systems is the efficiency they offer. Electronic retrieval is fast, as is electronic updating. Some electronic systems may permit automatic updating. For example, a system might be programmed to automatically move or purge files after a certain date.

Compared to manually filed hard copy records, computerized records take up little or no space, with the exception of the equipment and media required to store them. Another significant advantage of electronic records systems is their ability to generate reports and other types of documents using the data contained within each record.

Accounting Programs Help Crunch the Numbers

Most organizations use a computerized accounting program to handle all the accounting functions of the organization. There are several excellent software programs on the market designed to handle payroll, payables, receivables, financial statements, and other accounting functions at a reasonable cost. Customer billing programs can be purchased or designed to fit most types of organizations.

Questions?

What are the advantages and disadvantages of electronic storage?

Although there are many advantages to electronic records systems, there are also distinct disadvantages. The cost of purchasing computer equipment and programs is high, and many small organizations or businesses cannot afford the start-up costs. In addition, technology is changing so rapidly that programs may become out of date in as soon as three months. Some programs may have to be adapted to meet an organization's needs, and computer programming fees can add up quickly.

Because of the volume of information stored in an electronic system and the differing needs of organizations, security problems can also pose a challenge. **Information technology (IT)** staff or consultants may need to establish a system that uses security codes to protect confidential information.

Records management procedures, defined by records management staff, are extremely important to an electronic records system and can help to prevent loss or damage to records in the system. Human errors may cause slowdowns in productivity in all records systems, but mechanical breakdown of an electronic system can cause loss of information and loss of time. Electronic systems run the risk of being overloaded, which will result in the loss of information or scrambled records. Another worry comes from intentional damage brought about by a **computer virus,** which can infect computer files and programs, destroy information, and damage software programs.

Records Systems
- Manual
- Electronic
- Micrographic

Micrographic systems. Like electronic records systems, micrographic systems, in which documents are photographed, reduced to miniature size, and stored on high-resolution microfilm, require special equipment and training. Very large organizations, or organizations that produce quantities of records, may rely on micrographic records systems. For small organizations, it is generally not practical to use micrographics or optical disk technology to store records due to the cost for the volume of records stored.

All records systems have advantages and disadvantages, as summarized in Table 2-2. An organization weighs its needs, personnel, and financial resources before making decisions on changing or adapting its records systems.

Integrating Records Systems

Many organizations today have combined records systems, and the majority use computers in their daily office routines. Typewriters are the new dinosaurs now that the personal computer has become more powerful and more affordable. Even small organizations tend to have at least one computer, and large organizations often have a network connecting all computer terminals together into one system.

Questions?
What will be the records system of the future?

The **Internet** and **e-mail** have changed the way we communicate. Organizations can transmit information from one electronic system to another by telecommunications (see Figure 2-3). Information used in decision making is available faster because of the speed of transmitting information electronically instead of by postal services. A hard copy can be produced on either end of the transmission.

Table 2-2 Advantages and Disadvantages of Records Systems

Type of Records System	Advantages	Disadvantages
Manual	Easy access	Lack of storage space
	Easy to train personnel	Misfiling of records
	Hard copy readily available	Unqualified personnel
		High cost of supplies and equipment
Micrographic	Rapid retrieval	Start-up costs high
	Access to large volumes of data	Extensive employee training
	Reduces misfiled records	Programs must adapt to company needs
Electronic	Rapid retrieval	System breakdowns
	Records easy to update	System overload
	Reports easy to generate	Computer viruses can destroy information
	Access to volumes of data	Technology changes rapidly
	Multifunctional programs	Security problems
	Reduces misfiled records	Start-up costs high
	Saves space	Programs must be adapted to company needs
		Extensive employee training

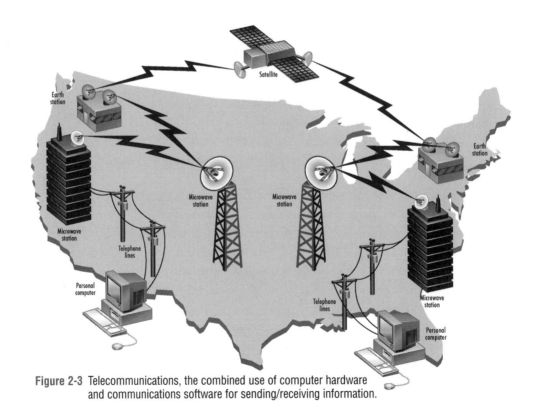

Figure 2-3 Telecommunications, the combined use of computer hardware and communications software for sending/receiving information.

Most information generated by computer can be stored on floppy diskettes, magnetic tapes, optical disks, or hard drives. Yet there still remain certain records that need to be retained in original hard copy form. Legal and fiscal documentation must be kept in manual systems for verification purposes and federal requirements. For example, documents such as property titles, tax forms, and receipts are items that should be retained in original form.

Questions?
Can records be maintained exclusively in electronic form?

Manual records systems will not be completely replaced by micrographic or electronic records systems in the future. Instead, most organizations will rely on an integrated records system in which all three systems interact to provide the most efficient and fastest records systems possible.

Records Management in the Real World

The Junior College

Draughons Junior College is a midsize college employing 16 administrators and 38 instructors. Approximately 500 students attend the school annually. The school uses several filing systems to help manage the large amounts of documentation it handles each year.

The junior college uses several records systems for each of its departments: the business office, the financial aid office, the admissions department, the academics office, the student placement office, the administrative offices, and the accounting department. Some of these records systems are integrated with the systems of other departments. However, some departments' records are used exclusively by that department and outside access is not allowed. All of the junior college's records are vital to the operation of the college and must be controlled to prevent misfiling and loss of records, as well as for legal documentation.

The business office contains several separate or combined filing systems. An individual file is created for each student, containing information such as application for admissions, documentation of previous schools, class registration forms, and booklists. These paper records are alphabetically filed and must be kept for a specified length of time according to federal law. For example, the business office is required to permanently store official transcripts on all past and present students. The college chooses to store these documents electronically. Student accounts are stored by computer for billing purposes, and all account transactions are entered into the computer. Hard copies of these electronically filed documents can easily be printed as needed. In addition, student ledger cards are filed alphabetically, showing all account transactions. The student information folder is kept for a specified time period after the student completes her or his education; once this time frame has elapsed, the junior college disposes of the contents of the folder.

Student records are used by all departments of the college. Chargeout procedures control access to the records by personnel outside the business office.

The college's financial aid office maintains alphabetical files with student information. This office keeps financial aid student information folders for five years, after which time they are disposed of. These files contain highly confidential financial information and so cannot be accessed by any other departments.

The academics office houses all instructors' records alphabetically. Copies of all class schedules, curriculum changes, and federal and state approvals are kept indefinitely, by subject or alphabetical systems. Course syllabuses are also housed in this office.

The administrative offices keep records alphabetically by year. The admissions department stores records alphabetically by student name, then chronologically by the semester or quarter the student is to begin classes, after which these files are moved to the business office.

The student placement office has several filing systems. Student resumes or applications are kept alphabetically in sequence, by part-time or full-time needs, or by program of study. Job orders are kept in chronological order or by type of position. When the job order is filled, it is filed in chronological order or alphabetically by company name. Once the student has found a position, the student's application is filed alphabetically.

The accounting department of the college uses both manual and electronic systems. Paid invoice records are stored chronologically by month and year on a computerized accounting system. Checks are processed manually and filed numerically. Posting is done electronically; a hard copy is stored chronologically by month and year, in accordance with government regulations that require all accounting records to be stored on a hard copy even if a computerized accounting system is used.

Legal documentation is required by federal government regulations to monitor all accounting procedures and college records. A computerized system makes processing information faster and more efficient; however, hard copy records still need to be stored by manual or micrographic systems.

For better understanding, review and reflect on the key points of this chapter.

Records are vital to the existence of an organization. Without proper records management, decisions may be hampered or incorrect decisions may cost an organization thousands of dollars.

There are four types of values placed on records. Records can have historical, operational, legal, or fiscal value.

Records are classified by their use or their destination. Records classified by their use are reference documents and transaction documents. Reference documents have historical value or explain how to do the work. Transaction documents are used in the daily operation of the organization. Records classified by their destination are either internal or external records. Internal documents are for the organization's own purposes and do not leave the organization. External documents include all correspondence sent from an organization to another location or correspondence received by the organization.

There are five steps in the life cycle of a record. From the time of *creation* through its *distribution* and *application*, the proper *maintenance* of a record is essential to its preservation. The final step, *disposition*, may be the transfer of a record either to archives or to disposal. The value of the record influences the decision to store or destroy documents.

Organizations may establish a centralized or decentralized filing system. Some organizations designate an area and assign staff to create a centralized filing system or records center. Alternately, some companies may prefer to house records in more than one location throughout the organization, creating a decentralized filing system.

Records are maintained in manual, electronic, and micrographic records systems. Organizations should weigh the advantages and disadvantages of all three systems before selecting an approach. Though manual systems are simple, they are very effective when original hard copies are important. Electronic and micrographic records systems provide work and space efficiencies, but generally cost more than a manual system. Many organizations rely on a combination of systems to manage their records.

True or False?
Rewrite each false item to make it a true statement.

1. Vital records are records essential to an organization and important to all areas of the organization.

2. A nonessential record should be retained in the organization's files for one year after its purpose has been served.

3. Records are classified by their use or their destination.

4. Transaction documents are used to conduct the everyday operations of the organization.

5. The life cycle of a record will vary depending on whether you are using manual, micrographic, or electronic records systems.

6. External documents are documents that are sent outside the organization to other organizations and individuals, and that are received from outside the organization.

7. Centralized filing systems designate all records to one location, usually called a records center.

8. Security codes are required to access databases of information in electronic centralized filing systems.

9. Decentralized filing systems house records at different locations throughout the organization.

10. Most organizations will combine manual records systems with some electronic records.

11. Micrographic records systems will be used in large organizations.

12. The cost of micrographic and electronic equipment is usually not a factor in deciding to upgrade manual records systems.

13. Electronic records systems will replace manual records systems in the near future.

14. Little or no training is necessary in learning micrographic and electronic records systems.

15. Most organizations will rely on integrated records systems, a combination of manual records systems with micrographic and electronic records systems, in the future.

Multiple Choice
Choose the best answer from those provided.

1. The four values placed on records in an organization are: a) historical, vital, legal, fiscal; b) historical, legal, fiscal, operational; c) legal, essential, vital, historical; d) legal, operational, vital, essential.

2. Records with long-term value that tell the story of an organization or are the basis of future managerial decisions are: a) historical records; b) operational records; c) legal records; d) fiscal records.

3. Records have four uses in business: a) historical, important, operational, useful; b) legal, vital, important, nonessential; c) vital, important, operational, useful; d) vital, important, useful, nonessential.

4. Vital records answer four questions about the organization: a) who, how, where, and when; b) who, what, when, and where; c) how, what, when, and where; d) what, if, when, and how much?

5. A procedural manual is an example of a/an: a) vital record; b) important record; c) useful record; d) nonessential record.

6. These records are necessary to the continuation of the organization and can be reproduced in case of destruction or loss at a great cost: a) vital records; b) important records; c) useful records; d) nonessential records.

7. If you lost your electric bill, you could contact the electric company and they would send you a duplicate bill as a replacement. This type of record is needed in the daily operation of a business or your personal life and, if lost, may cause inconvenience or delay. It is called a/an: a) vital record; b) important record; c) useful record; d) nonessential record.

8. An example of a nonessential record is: a) a cancelled payroll check; b) a letter from an insurance company quoting new insurance premium rates; c) a memo to all employees regarding the Christmas party; d) articles of incorporation of the organization.

9. Records may be classified in two ways: a) need and destination; b) use and destination; c) use and disposition; d) type of system and value.

10. Records classified by how they are used are called: a) reference and knowledge documents; b) transaction and operational documents; c) reference and transaction documents; d) reference and procedural documents.

11. General correspondence, fiscal documents, legal documents, and daily operational documents are examples of: a) reference documents; b) historical documents; c) knowledge documents; d) transaction documents.

12. Documents explaining how and why procedures are done by the organization or containing information vital to the operation of the organization are: a) reference documents; b) transaction documents; c) knowledge documents; d) legal documents.

13. The five steps in the life cycle of a record are: a) creation, distribution, use, maintenance, filing; b) keying, sending, using, filing, archiving; c) creation, distribution, use, maintenance, disposition; d) keying, distributing, using, maintaining, disposing.

14. Step four in the life cycle of a record is maintenance. Maintenance is: a) preserving a record properly from its creation through its distribution and use; b) preserving a record with historical value when it is sent to archives; c) keeping records in good condition in their file folders; d) keeping the records center clean.

15. Records may be stored in two types of filing systems: a) in-location and off-location filing systems; b) centralized and decentralized filing systems; c) on-site and off-site filing systems; d) satellite and centralized filing systems.

Terms to Know

Write definitions of these terms to increase your knowledge of the records management field.

application
chargeout program
computer virus
creation
database
database program
distribution
external
fiscal records

historical records
important records
information technology
  (IT)
internal
legal records
maintenance
nonessential records
operational records

records center
reference documents
soft copy
spreadsheet program
transaction documents
useful records
vital records
word processing program

Make a Connection

Write or discuss your response to each question.

1. Explain the four uses of records in an organization. Is any one use more important than another? Defend your position.

2. What are the four categories of value placed on records? How would you rank them in importance?

3. Identify the types of records classified by their use. Give an example of each.

4. Explain the difference between an internal and an external document. Give an example of each and state whether you believe records management systems need to differ based on where the record ends up.

5. Discuss the advantages and disadvantages of centralized and decentralized storage systems.

6. List and define the three types of records systems used in businesses, and give examples of each.

7. Explain the problems that can occur in each of the records systems.

The following activities require a computer and Internet connectivity.

1. Visit a search engine on the Internet, using the list below as a guide. Search the topic of *records management* and then link to at least three of the sites provided in your search results. What kinds of information did you discover? Share at least one example of useful information. If you have access to a printer, print one or more pages from any site you find particularly interesting to share with your class.

   www.altavista.com
   www.excite.com
   www.go.com
   www.goto.com
   www.google.com
   www.hotbot.com
   www.lycos.com
   www.yahoo.com

2. Visit a search engine to locate information about a database program. Find out what the program can do and how much it costs.

Thinking It Through

Dig deeper to apply what you have learned.

1. Have you ever lost an item that included important records, such as a receipt, your checkbook, or perhaps a school notebook? Think of a time you were inconvenienced by your own lack of records management. How might you have avoided the problems that arose by losing the item?

2. Review the advantages and disadvantages of the manual, electronic, and micrographic systems provided in Table 2-2. Select one of these three systems and apply it to a fictional business. Generate real-world examples that bring these pros and cons to life.

3. Find out what kind of records management systems are used by the school you attend. Does the school have a records center? Are manual, electronic, and micrographic systems used and integrated? Report your findings.

Evaluating Manual Records Systems

3

Determine How Well a System Works, then Seek to Improve It

What's stored in this chapter?
Read on to learn...

- 📁 How to evaluate an existing records system
- 📁 When to change an existing records system
- 📁 How to conduct a records inventory
- 📁 The difference between perpetual and periodic records transfer
- 📁 How to use and modify control procedures in a records system
- 📁 How to develop guides for the control of forms

Nearly every organization—whether it is a nonprofit agency, a small business, or a multinational corporation—has some form of records system in place. The range and complexity of systems vary widely, depending on organizational size and business needs. The amount of money dedicated to records management equipment and personnel will also affect the type of system an organization adopts.

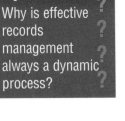

Questions?

Why is effective records management always a dynamic process?

For companies of all shapes and sizes, effective records management is always a dynamic process, requiring flexible and innovative solutions. A records system that worked well last year, or even last week, may not be adequate to keep pace with a growing business. A filing system that  doubles in size may need a space-saving alternative. For this reason, a company's records system should be periodically evaluated to determine whether it permits information to be properly stored and rapidly retrieved. Recommendations for change will flow from the evaluation.

Assessing the Status Quo: Is the System Working? Can It Be Improved?

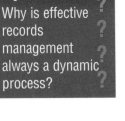

Questions?

How do you conduct an analysis of a records system?

The best way to determine whether a records system is working effectively is to conduct an analysis of that system. One efficient method for this process is to appoint a **system analysis team** representing all levels of personnel from top management to general employees.
Together, the team can establish study objectives, a study plan, and workable time frame for the assessment.

The analysis should evaluate the types of records created, received, and stored, and their corresponding retention schedules. The system analysis team is charged with collecting information and making recommendations based on the findings. The analysis should result in a formal report that describes the present records system, a review of any problems, recommendations for changes, a description of the new system, and the cost of implementation. Alternately, if the present records system is adequate, the report should document these findings.

The tools for assessing an existing records system include questionnaires or interviews and a survey of current records.

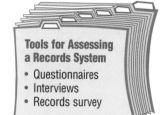

Tools for Assessing a Records System
- Questionnaires
- Interviews
- Records survey

Questionnaires or interviews. Based on available time and resources, the system analysis team may decide to administer questionnaires or conduct individual interviews to gather input from the people who use the present records system. To collect useful data, the questions contained in either format should be structured to elicit specific, fact-based responses rather than opinions. Questions might include:

1. What is the process and turnaround time for requesting information?
2. How effective is the present chargeout system? Has the system ever failed?
3. How does the present records system meet the organization's records needs?
4. Are you satisfied with the current records system? Why or why not?
5. Explain any areas that need restructuring in the records system. What changes would you recommend? Why?

A records survey. A physical survey of the records stored throughout the organization helps the team identify all facets of the existing records management system. A thorough records survey will examine the following:

When evaluating an existing records management system, remember the familiar adage, "If it ain't broke, don't fix it!"

- The types of records created and received by the organization.
- Where the records are housed.
- Existing filing arrangements (alphabetic, subject, geographic, and numeric).
- Retention and disposal records schedules.

Steps for Evaluating an Existing Records Systems or Setting Up a New System

When you want to improve or establish a records system, take time to evaluate what is currently being used. Appoint a system analysis team to complete the following tasks:

1. Establish study objectives, a study plan, and a workable time frame for the assessment.
2. Collect data from employees through questionnaires and personal interviews.
3. Identify the types of records created, received, and stored.
4. List the location where the records are stored in the organization.
5. Study the retention schedule of records to learn what records are kept indefinitely, what records are transferred, and corresponding disposal schedules.
6. Study the data collected and make recommendations to management about the records system.
7. Document the study's findings in a report containing recommendations along with a plan of implementation.

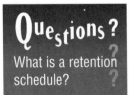

Before changing a records system, take time to understand the people who use the system and how new procedures will affect their work processes. Remember that people need time to adjust to change and accept new ideas from an outside source.

Que**stions**?

What is a retention schedule?

Retention Schedules: The Blueprint for Keeping or Tossing Records

Most records have a shelf life, meaning that at some point in time they lose their value and can be disposed of. To keep track of this information—helping to prevent unauthorized destruction of records as well as accumulation of obsolete records—many organizations maintain a detailed **retention schedule**. A retention schedule (see Table 3-1) lists all of the types of records kept by the organization, specifying the length of time records must be retained. The schedule should be clear and concise so that it is understood by the office staff.

Development of the retention schedule involves communication among the people who use the records as well as the administrator and the records manager. The retention schedule should be periodically updated to ensure its accuracy. Records have three identifiable dispositions in retention (see Figure 3-1):

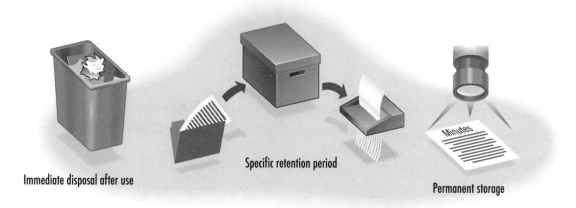

Figure 3-1 Disposition of Records in Retention

1. **Immediate disposal after use.** These records can be discarded immediately after use. For example, a memo regarding a companywide software installation can be disposed of after the installation has occurred.

2. **A specific retention period.** Records of this nature may be moved from active files to inactive files. For example, accounts payable records are generally moved to inactive storage at the end of each fiscal year; once their retention date expires, these records are discarded by shredding, burning, or some other acceptable disposal method (depending on the nature of the documents).

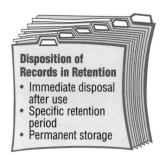

3. **Permanent storage.** These records may be maintained in a company storage center, a privately owned off-site storage center, or on microform or electronic media. For example, documentation of the organization's minutes of corporate meetings must be retained for the duration of the organization and must be properly saved.

Table 3-1 Sample Retention Schedule for a Business

RETENTION SCHEDULE

Record Category	Record Title	Retention Period
Administration	Annual Reports	Permanent
	Audit Reports	3 years
	Correspondence	3 years
	Insurance Policies	3 years after expiration
	Investments, Bonds and Stocks	3 years from due date of sale
	Journals	3-6 years after audit
	Leases	6 years after termination
	Licenses	6 years after expiration
	Minutes of Board Meetings	Permanent
	Mortgages	Permanent
Accounting/Finance	Accounts Payable	3-6 years after audit
	Accounts Receivable	3-6 years after audit
	Budgets	6 years after execution
	Certificates of Deposit	6 years after audit
	Cancelled Checks	6 years after audit
	Contracts	6 years after audit
	Depreciation	6-10 years after audit
	Employment Tax Records	3 years after due date of tax return
	Fixed Assets	3 years after date of sale
	Ledgers	3-6 years
	Payroll Documents	3 years after due date of tax return
	Purchase Orders	3 years after final payment
Personnel	Accident Reports	Permanent
	Employee Personnel Folders	3-6 years after termination of employment
	Retirement Records	Permanent

Keeping Track with a Records Inventory

A physical inventory of an organization's records must be conducted before a retention schedule can be developed or an existing retention schedule evaluated. Records should be appraised for immediate and future usefulness, as well as archival purposes. Consultation with legal advisors is necessary to ensure that the retention schedule abides by federal, state, and local laws governing the retention of records and also to protect the company in the event of future litigation.

Conducting a **records use analysis** as part of a records inventory helps identify how often files are actually used. It is a relatively simple process that can be done by marking each filing cabinet drawer with a tag or label describing the drawer contents. The description should include the type of files (alphabetic, subject, and so on), name series, and the years of coverage. Each

Questions?

What is the value of a physical records inventory?

time a file is removed from the drawer for use, a mark is made on the tag. A clear pattern of record usage will emerge in four to six weeks of study.

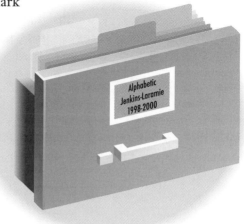

The analysis should review **turnaround time** in the existing records system. Turnaround time has several meanings:

1. It can refer to the time it takes an individual to find the requested file or document and retrieve it when a record is requested.

2. It can be the time it takes to inspect, index, code, sort, and store a record.

3. It can be the period of time a record is allowed to be checked out of the records center.

📄 Looking for a Record? Check the Records Procedures Manual

A **records procedures manual** is a "how-to" reference book explaining a company's records system, procedures to be used in the records system, and the types of records stored. The procedures manual acts as an instructional device explaining how records are to be processed by the employees. The procedures manual can be used to train new employees and serves as an excellent reference manual. A records procedures manual may include the following:

- Company organizational chart
- General records policies
- Descriptions of existing records systems
- Types of forms used
- Chargeout procedures
- Records retention schedules
- Employee duties and responsibilities
- Rules for filing

From the inventory analysis of the records, you can determine whether the records are active or inactive and the location where the records will be retained. In general, the following guidelines apply to the use of active versus inactive storage:

Elements of an Inventory
- Records use analysis
- Turnaround time
- Active versus inactive storage

Active storage. Records in active storage are used a minimum of two times a month. These records must be easy to access at any given time. Most records will remain in active storage for one to two years, but the retention period will vary depending on the type of records and their use in the office.

Inactive storage. Records in inactive storage may be kept on-site or at an off-site location. Many organizations do not have adequate storage space and will keep inactive records at an off-site storage facility. Inactive records are usually stored in labeled corrugated, fiberboard boxes or storage drawers. The labels on the end of the storage container include the contents of the file box and the date of storage and disposal (see Figure 3-2).

Figure 3-2 Inactive Files Boxed for Storage

Records archive. Most organizations have certain records that must be kept permanently. These valuable records are stored in the organization's archives, housed in a secure and safe location within the organization to prevent water and fire damage.

Records on the Move

When records are moved from active to inactive storage, a system must be implemented for the transfer of the records. There are two **records transfer** methods used by businesses.

Perpetual transfer. The **perpetual transfer** method is a continual transfer process that occurs on a weekly, monthly, or bimonthly basis. Records are always being moved to inactive storage or disposal.

Periodic transfer. The **periodic transfer** method designates specific time periods for the transfer of records. The organization may transfer records semiannually or annually, depending on the volume of records to be relocated. Whenever possible, periodic transfer of records is best scheduled during slower periods in the office work. In most organizations, management prefers to determine the time for the records transfer.

Maintaining Control of Important Records

All records systems must have **control procedures** to ensure an accurate and secure records system. Chargeout controls help prevent loss of records and should be evaluated periodically to determine effectiveness.

A records system is like a library and should have similar controls. When you check out a library book, you are asked to return the book by a specified date. Every record taken from the records system should be checked out and checked back into the center upon its return. A charge-out time period should be established based on business needs. For example, five days may be determined to be the acceptable maximum time limit for "borrowing" a record from the records center. On the fifth day, a reminder sent to the individual holding the record can help stimulate prompter returns.

As a precaution, do not allow confidential records to be checked out overnight.

🗎 Tips for Keeping Tabs on Important Records

- Limit access to authorized personnel only.
- Lock filing cabinets at the end of each business day.
- Store indexes of the subject, numeric, and geographic filing systems where unauthorized personnel are unable to access the information.
- Require authorization from management before confidential records are released.

Keeping the Number of Forms Under Control

How many times have you completed a form that asks the same information more than once? How often have you needed to complete two or three forms that request some of the same information? Not only is it time consuming for the individual to supply the same information multiple times, it is similarly time consuming and expensive for an organization to process the same information repeatedly.

Reducing the number of unnecessary forms used by a business allows better control of the filing system and reduces paperwork. Forms cost money to produce, adding to overhead and lowering the revenue retained by the organization.

Increasingly, **electronic forms** (see Figure 3-3) are a desirable way for businesses to gather information. Individuals can complete the forms at their desktop computers and then transmit their responses electronically (by internal e-mail). A database collects the information, which can be easily accessed and used for business purposes.

Most organizations have many types of forms that overlap one another. This may happen when individual departments develop forms relating to departmental tasks and do not consult with other departments to see if a form already exists for this purpose. Often forms can be combined together with minimal adjustments to each specialized form.

Frequently, the volume of forms handled by an organization can be reduced by a careful review of forms usage across departments. Ask the following questions when conducting a forms review:

1. Is the form necessary?
2. Does the form duplicate another form?
3. Can several forms be combined together for better usage to the organization?
4. Is the form easy to complete?
5. Are duplicate copies of the form needed?
6. How many copies are needed for distribution?
7. What is the form's distribution cycle?

MANUFACTURING REQUEST	
DATE/TIME TO PURCHASING	January 23, 2001
DUE IN WAREHOUSE	March 1, 2001
FROM	Jane Smith
EDITOR	Robert Brown

TITLE	Life and Times in London
SEGMENT/ITEM	Text
ISBN	0-12345-6789-X
C/N	01110
ORDER NUMBER	12345
YOU ARE RECEIVING	Text files and pagination grid

PROGRAM MANUAL		COVER	
SIZE	8 3/8 x 10 7/8	SIZE	same
STOCK	50# white offset	STOCK	12 pt C1S Layflatt
PAGES	264	COLORS	Process
COLORS	Process	BINDING STYLE	Perfect
PERFORATE	No	FINISH	Film Lam
HALF TONES LINE ART BLEEDS SCREENS	YES YES YES YES YES	COIL BINDING	POSITION: TYPE COLOR: VENDOR
PROOF TYPE	Digital color bluelines	PROOF TYPE	Matchprint
PROOFS DUE	January 15, 2001	PROOFS DUE	January 15, 2001
PRINT VENDOR	Smithfield Press	PRINT VENDOR	Smithfield Press
EDP VENDOR	Joan Silver	EDP VENDOR	Joan Silver
PRINT PROCESS	Film	PRINT PROCESS	Film
SPECIAL INSTRUCTIONS Last 16 page signature (index) to come at a later date.		SPECIAL INSTRUCTIONS We require 10 additional covers to be sent to Joan Silver	

Figure 3-3 Example of an Electronic Form

Records Management in the Real World

Dora Sharpe

Dora Sharpe worked with many types of records throughout her 37-year career at Johnson Cabinet Company. She began in 1949 as a personnel clerk for the small independent furniture manufacturing company in Nashville, Tennessee. During her tenure in the personnel department, she cross-trained and learned the various duties of the accounting department. Dora transferred to accounting as the payroll clerk and eventually became the accounting manager. For a small company, Johnson Cabinet Company kept many types of records.

In the personnel department, Dora filed all employee records alphabetically. The furniture maker employed between 300 and 500 people. Each division foreman kept an address book of his employees in which he updated addresses and telephone numbers. Changes were turned in to the personnel department monthly so they could be documented.

The accounting department was responsible for working with the personnel department in handling the payroll. Employees used a time clock for logging their hours on time cards with employee names and numbers at the top. After payroll was figured manually on a weekly basis, the time cards would be filed numerically by employee numbers rather than by employee names.

Cost accounting records, used for inventory purposes, were kept numerically. Each furniture style (e.g., "Lillian Russell") was given a letter and numeric code (e.g., LR-101). The company made 10 or 11 styles of furniture at a time.

All accounts payable records were filed by the date the account was paid. Each month had a guide; bills were filed by the day they were paid and placed in folders with that date.

The sales department kept three types of records: alphabetic by company name, numeric by order number, and alphabetic by salesperson's name. The accounting department worked with the sales department in tracking each salesperson's commissions and accounts receivable. For Johnson Cabinet Company to get paid for the furniture it sold to its dealers, the company depended on the sales department to supply this information in order to bill the furniture companies. For the salespeople to receive a paycheck, the sales department supplied the accounting department with the amount of sales for their commission checks.

Dora retired as company treasurer in 1986, when Johnson Cabinet Company was sold to a large furniture manufacturer in North Carolina. Dora is an example of learning all you can about a company and its job opportunities, and then working your way to the top.

For better understanding, review and reflect on the key points of this chapter.

Organizations can determine whether a records system is working effectively by conducting a records use analysis. This procedure generally includes the assignment of a system analysis team to collect data and make recommendations to management.

A records retention schedule provides guidelines for maintaining records. This type of schedule lists all of the records kept by the organization, with the length of time they will retained. Before the retention schedule is developed, a physical inventory of the organization's records can help to determine how often the records are actually used in the course of business.

Records can be physically located in active storage, inactive storage, and archives. Once a record is no longer useful to the organization, it can be disposed of by burning, shredding, or other acceptable means.

There are two methods to transfer records from active to inactive storage or archives. Perpetual transfer is the ongoing transfer method, while periodic transfer designates specific time periods for records transfer.

Control procedures ensure an accurate and secure records system. Chargeout controls prevent loss of records and act as a checkout device similar to checking out a library book. A designated return period helps to ensure the timely return of important documents.

Confidential records require greater control measures. For example, an employee may require authorization from management in order to access a confidential record.

A records procedures manual explains the procedures used in the records system and the types of records stored. The manual serves as a "how-to" reference book and is particularly useful for training new employees.

Most organizations can reduce the number of forms in use. A review of the existing forms can be included in the evaluation of the existing records system. Reducing the number of files needed to do business can help to prevent overloading of the file system and can actually save the organization money.

True or False?
Rewrite each false item to make it a true statement.

1. Periodic evaluations of a records system ensure that the system is working properly.

2. Before you change the current records system, you must review the system thoroughly.

3. The system analysis team will be selected by management from all areas of the organization.

4. A physical inventory of the organization's records must be conducted before a retention schedule can be developed or an in-place retention schedule evaluated.

5. A records use analysis is conducted to see how often the files are being used.

6. A retention schedule is a permanent list of all records kept by the organization, the length of time they must be retained, and site of their transfer or disposal.

7. Records stored in archives are always sent to off-site storage facilities.

8. Periodic transfer of records designates specific time periods for the transfer.

9. All records systems must have control procedures to ensure accuracy and security.

10. Access to the records center should be unrestricted to all personnel in the organization.

11. Authorization must be obtained from management before a confidential record can be released from the records center.

12. A procedures manual can act as an instructional device for new employees.

13. A procedures manual is a "how-to" reference book explaining the records system, types of records stored, and procedures used in the records system.

14. Most organizations do not have enough forms and need to develop more forms for better control of the organization.

15. A form should be designed for maximum ease of use and should not duplicate other forms in the organization.

Multiple Choice
Choose the best answer from those provided.

1. Accident Reports would be retained: a) 1 year; b) 3 years; c) 6 years; d) permanently

2. The period of time a record is allowed to be checked out of the records center is the _____ time. a) borrow; b) checkout; c) turnaround; d). chargeout.

3. A permanent list of all groups of records kept by the organization, specifying the length of time records must be retained and the site of all records transfer or disposition, is called a: a) retention list; b) records category; c) records program; d) retention schedule.

4. The group of personnel selected to evaluate a records system is called the: a) study group; b) system analysis team; c) management study team; d) system group team.

5. When a records system is being evaluated, data will be collected from personnel in the organization through the following sources: a) interviews and reports; b) questionnaires and reports; c) interviews and questionnaires; d) surveys and reports.

6. Before a retention schedule can be developed, records should be appraised for immediate and future usefulness by studying their use. This is called a/an: a) physical inventory; b) random counting; c) audit; d) itemization listing.

7. This will be conducted over a period of four to six weeks as part of the physical inventory to see how often the files are being used. It is called a: a) records count; b) records audit; c) records breakdown; d) records use analysis.

8. The three storage dispositions for records are: a) active, temporary, and inactive storage; b) active, temporary, and archive storage; c) active, inactive, and archive storage, d) temporary, inactive, and archive storage.

9. If a record is used a minimum of two times a month, it is considered to be a/an: a) inactive record; b) semi-active record; c) archive record; d) active record.

10. Copies of an organization's minutes of corporate meetings must be retained for the duration of the organization. These records would be stored as a/an: a) inactive record; b) semi-active record; c) archive record; d) active record.

11. There are two methods of transfer by which businesses move records from active to inactive storage. They are: a) constant and occasional transfer; b) ongoing and occasional transfer; c) perpetual and periodic transfer; d) ongoing and sporadic transfer.

12. The records transfer method that is a continual process occurring on a daily, weekly, bimonthly, or monthly basis is called: a) constant transfer; b) perpetual transfer; c) ongoing transfer; d) nonstop transfer.

13. The records transfer method that designates specific time periods for the transfer of records is called: a) sporadic transfer; b) occasional transfer; c) periodic transfer; d) intermittent transfer.

14. Records systems use preventative measures to ensure accurate and secure records. These are: a) control procedures; b) lending procedures; c) security procedures; d) checkout procedures.

15. The "how to" reference book that explains the records system, procedures used in the records system, instructional devices for new employees, and the types of records stored is called a: a) records system guidebook; b) records system handbook; c) records system rulebook; d) records procedures manual.

ON THE JOB

Terms to Know

Write definitions of these terms to increase your knowledge of the records management field.

control procedures
electronic forms
inactive storage
periodic transfer
perpetual transfer
records archive
records disposition

records inventory
records procedures manual
records use analysis
retention period
retention schedule
system analysis team

Make a Connection

Write or discuss your response to each question.

1. Why is it necessary to evaluate an existing records system? Describe a situation that would warrant the expense of a records system analysis.

2. What does the system analysis team do to perform the analysis? Why is it important to have a cross-functional team (people representing different areas and levels within the organization)?

3. What is a retention schedule? Why is it important?

4. What information would you need to determine whether a record is stored on site or off site, in active or inactive storage? List advantages and disadvantages of each storage method for an infrequently used record.

5. Make an argument for the disposal of all memos and documentation related to the recent renovation of the company cafeteria, then argue the position that everything should be maintained in inactive storage.

6. Why do some records need to be stored permanently? Give examples of business records that generally require permanent storage.

7. Briefly explain the preventive measures used in controlling a records system.

8. Why is it necessary to control the forms developed and used in an organization?

The following activities require a computer and Internet connectivity.

1. You have been assigned to a system analysis team. How might a computer be useful to the analysis process? Describe the ways you might use electronic communications to facilitate the analysis.

2. List any forms you have completed online. Did you find it a more efficient way to provide the information? Were there any limitations or difficulties? Go online to find and print an example of an electronic form.

3. Your office is running out of storage space for the records it must maintain. Conduct an online investigation of off-site records storage centers in your community. Write and deliver to your class a report on costs, delivery systems, capacity, and any other pertinent information you discover in your research.

4. Visit the home pages of two or three of the popular search engines. See what guidelines you can find on writing a procedures manual. Compare and contrast the differences in linkages and information available through the different engines. Which would you rate as the most helpful in seeking out the information you need?

5. Through your state's Web site, research legislation enacted by your state regarding records and their retention schedules. Write a report that outlines concisely the major points of these local laws.

Thinking It Through

Dig deeper to apply what you have learned.

1. You have been promoted to the position of administrative manager. One of your departments is the records center that houses all of the organization's records except the personnel records. The previous administrative manager did not understand the importance of a good records system, and the department reflects this attitude. Several employees in the records center demonstrate poor job skills and disregard the established rules of records management. How would you, as the newly appointed records manager, correct the situation in the records center?

2. The top management of your organization has requested that you oversee the evaluation of the records management department. As the evaluation team leader, you must select the team members and establish the objectives of the evaluation. Who would you select as team members? What objectives would you set and how would you set them? List the questions you would ask in questionnaires and personal interviews.

3. All businesses use a variety of forms in their daily operation. Think of all the forms used where you work or contact a business about the type of forms they use. Make a list of all the forms used by the organization. Review the forms used and answer the following questions:

   - Are all the forms used by the organization necessary to the operation of the organization?
   - Could any of the forms be redesigned for better usage, or even discarded?
   - Where and how are the forms stored in the organization?

Manual Filing Systems

4

Options for Filing Information by Hand

What's stored in this chapter?
Read on to learn...

- The six types of manual filing systems
- How to store records
- Principles for indexing records
- When and how to cross-reference a record
- How to implement a record chargeout system
- Strategies for searching for a misfiled record

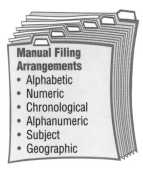
What is the solution for the mountains of records that organizations accumulate over time? What should administrative assistants and other office workers do with the letters, meeting minutes, research, resumes, invoices, and other documentation that land on their desks, begging to be maintained in an orderly fashion until future reference? If an organization has decided it needs to maintain paper records—and most do, despite our increasing use of electronic storage—the question is how best to store the records for easy retrieval. As you will learn by reading this chapter, there are a number of manual filing options from which to choose.

How an organization decides to file its records will depend on the type of business it conducts as well as the information contained in a typical record. Many organizations establish multiple filing systems for different types of information. For example, a medical office may file all of its patient records by the patient's name (or perhaps an assigned patient number) in one set of file drawers, and use a separate file drawer in which to file accounts payable files arranged by vendor. The number of filing arrangements increases with the complexity of the information handled by the organization.

Manual Filing Arrangements
- Alphabetic
- Numeric
- Chronological
- Alphanumeric
- Subject
- Geographic

The Range of Manual Filing Arrangements

There are six types of manual filing arrangements used in today's offices: alphabetic, numeric, chronological, alphanumeric, subject, and geographic. All manual filing arrangements use the same filing procedures, equipment, and supplies. The manual systems differ according to what aspect of the record will guide the filing, such as a company or individual name attached to the record; a form number, date, or case number; the topic of the record; or perhaps the region to which it pertains.

The decision to select a particular manual filing arrangement should be driven by how the organization needs to access the information. It may be quite obvious, based on the types of records being filed. Why file receipts by type of merchandise when each is marked by a date of purchase? Why store meeting minutes by date when meetings are centered on specific company projects? The variety of manual filing systems provides options that range from basic to complex. Alphabetic and chronological arrangements are the simplest. The others may be more complex, yet offer distinct advantages for specific types of filing needs.

Alphabetic filing arrangements. You are probably familiar with this method of arranging information. If you attended a typical elementary school, you may have been assigned a seat based on alphabetic order—at least until the teacher learned everyone's name. Beyond that experience, you have surely relied on alphabetic filing in other aspects of everyday life. For example, to look up a telephone number or to locate a street on a city map, you refer to an alphabetic index.

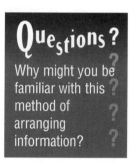

Why might you be familiar with this method of arranging information?

In alphabetic filing, all records are stored in **dictionary order**, from A to Z. Alphabetic records are filed by a person's name, company name, or subject name. An alphabetic filing system contains a **primary guide** for each letter of the alphabet. Individual folders that correspond to that letter follow the primary guide. For example, the primary letter A guide precedes all files beginning with the letter A, which are placed in alphabetic order. **General record folders**, one for each letter of the alphabet, are designed to hold miscellaneous records that do not have an individual folder. The general folder belongs behind all of the files related to the corresponding letter of the alphabet. For example, the general A folder will be the last folder before the primary B folder (see Figure 4-1).

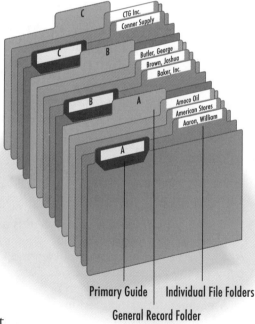

Figure 4-1 Files arranged alphabetically, with general record folder at the end of each letter.

The general folder is a "catch-all" folder for documents that do not warrant an individual folder. All documents in the general file folder are filed alphabetically. If there is more than one document for the same person, company, or subject, the documents are filed in date order, with the most recent record placed in the front.

Once six or more related items accumulate, you can remove them from the general folder and create an individual file folder.

While filing alphabetically is the most common and perhaps the simplest filing arrangement, it still requires study and practice to implement correctly. To help records management professionals maintain alphabetic records systems more efficiently, the Association of Records Managers and Administrators (ARMA) has established rules for alphabetic filing. ARMA, the professional organization for records management personnel, is respected by most organizations that desire a unified records systems. You will learn about the ARMA rules in Chapter 6.

Create individual folders when you have a minimum of six pieces of correspondence on a particular person, company, or subject. Place items that do not meet this minimum in the general folder corresponding to the appropriate letter of the alphabet.

Table 4-1 Alphabetic Filing Arrangements

ALPHABETIC FILING

Advantages	Disadvantages
Easy to learn and use Easy to check for misfiled records Direct access; no need for an index Fast storage and retrieval Less training time and actual filing time	Files are not secure or confidential

Sorting Tips

1. Remove paper clips holding the records together. Paper clips have a tendency to add additional records to the clipped records and can result in misfiled records.
2. Staple records together in the upper right corner. This gives the records support when removing the record from the folder and keeps other records from getting stuck between the stapled records when filing a new record.
3. Tape small items of information on an 8½ x 11″ sheet of paper. This will prevent the information from getting lost in the folder.
4. Mend torn records before inserting them into the folder.
5. Records that are larger than folder size should be carefully folded to fit the folder.

Numeric filling arrangements. To the phone company, you are just a number. That is, your telephone number tracks all of the information related to your account. Like the phone company, many organizations, such as hospital records centers, place emphasis on assigned numbers, which become the basis for their internal filing arrangements.

In numeric filing arrangements, records are assigned numbers and filed in numeric sequence (see Figure 4-2). Invoices, vouchers, and purchase orders have preprinted numbers and are examples of records that are filed numerically. Another reason for numeric filing may be confidentiality. Confidential records can be stored by number instead of a name, to protect the identity of the people involved. Most legal offices use case numbers instead of names when filing records, and maintain an alphabetic index listing the business or individual name that corresponds to the case number. Employee personnel records may be assigned an employee number and filed accordingly, or filed by the employee's social security number, also to protect the information.

You might be thinking that a numeric arrangement would be difficult to search, since numbers are harder to remember. For example, how do you find the case file for Oliver Hernandez if it was stored under case number 200488, a number you have long since forgotten? Many organizations that use numeric filing will simultaneously maintain an **alphabetic index** to aid storage and retrieval. You will learn more about various specialized numeric arrangements available for office use in Chapter 8.

Questions?
How can numeric filing provide confidentiality?

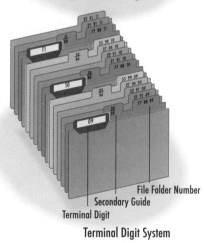

Serial Arrangement

File Folder Number
Secondary Guide
Terminal Digit

Terminal Digit System

Figure 4-2 Files Arranged Numerically

Table 4-2 Numeric Filing Arrangements

Advantages	Disadvantages
Easy to expand	Must check alphabetic index for record number before storing
Prenumbered records are easy to sort	More time consuming; requires a double sort
Lower equipment costs	Maintenance time of alphabetic index required
Confidential	
Advanced labeling for new files	
Easy to set up a retention and disposal schedule	
Cross-referencing appears on index card, not in filing system	
Numbers are easier to read than names, subjects, or titles	

Chronological filing arrangements. In some organizations, *when* a record is needed is more important than *what* the record contains. Chronological filing, in which records are arranged based on the date the record is needed, makes the most sense. A chronological file features month guides, and records are placed behind each month guide in date order (see Figure 4-3).

Figure 4-3 Files Arranged Chronologically

Chronological arrangements serve as a memory helper. An administrative assistant or administrator may use a **tickler file** as a reminder device for assignments or appointments. An example of a good tickler file is a file box containing 3 x 5" cards separated by guide cards for each month, as well as numbered guides from 1 to 31 for each day of the month (see Figure 4-4). Include a guide card for "future years," for items that will be of importance in 12 months or more. Each record assigned to the tickler file is placed behind the date the item will be needed. The trick with a tickler file is to use it! To use a tickler file effectively, look at the contents of your tickler file each day to remain aware of what needs to be accomplished.

Questions?
What is the value of a tickler file?

Review a pending file at least twice weekly to check the status of the items on hold.

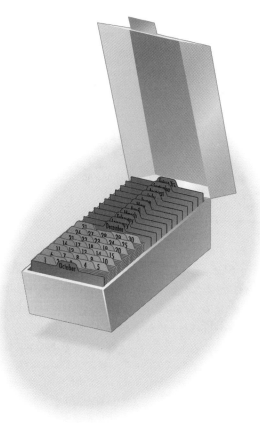

Figure 4-4 A Tickler File

A **pending or suspense file** is a special chronological filing system used as a temporary checklist for items currently being processed. Once the outstanding item has been processed, then the item in the pending file should be released or returned to the regular filing system. A pending file should be reviewed at least twice weekly to check the status of the items on hold.

A **reading file** is also a special chronological system used by administrative assistants and administrators for easy access to copies of daily correspondence. Correspondence records are placed in the reading file by date for a specified time period decided by office personnel. The most recent items are placed at the front of the file. This system is used in-house and generally the records are destroyed after three to six months.

Table 4-3 Chronological Filing Arrangements

CHRONOLOGICAL FILING	
Advantages	**Disadvantages**
Fast retrieval of information Memory aid for pending and in-process documents	Time-consuming activity

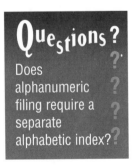

Questions?

Does alphanumeric filing require a separate alphabetic index?

Alphanumeric filing arrangements. Alphanumeric arrangements are similar to an outline; they use a combination of letters and numbers. This type of system organizes records alphabetically by subject, with subdivisions for each main subject assigned a number. The main subject guide is followed by numbered subdivision guides (see Figure 4-5). Expansion is easy because of intentional gaps (skips) in the number sequence. To make it easier to find and correctly file information, records personnel generally create an **alphabetic index** to correspond to the numeric coding for each subject.

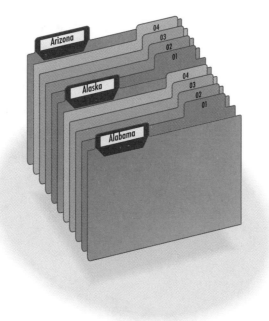

Figure 4-5 Files Arranged Alphanumerically

Table 4-4 Alphanumeric Filing
Arrangements

ALPHANUMERIC FILING	
Advantages	**Disadvantages**
Easy to expand	Difficult to learn Alphabetic index must be consulted

Subject filing arrangements. Subject filing refers to records arranged by topics or categories instead of individual or company names (examples: equipment, repair companies, supply companies, and so on). Subject filing uses either dictionary or encyclopedic order for storage. The **dictionary arrangement** is the simple A-to-Z storage method. The **encyclopedic arrangement** is a method of ordering records by main topic with subdivisions filed alphabetically behind the first letter of the main topic (see Figure 4-6).

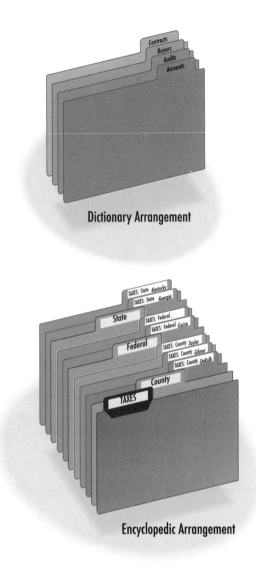

Dictionary Arrangement

Encyclopedic Arrangement

Figure 4-6 Files Arranged by Subject

Like alphanumeric filing systems, subject filing systems require a general alphabetic index. The alphabetic index helps the filer to determine the subject or topic name and provides uniformity in subject titles. This alphabetic index is consulted whenever a record is filed in subject systems.

Table 4-5 Subject Filing Arrangements

SUBJECT FILING	
Advantages	**Disadvantages**
All information on a topic is grouped together for easy research Most subjects are easy to remember	Alphabetic index must be maintained More expensive than other filing systems because of training time required Requires a double sort, first by alphabet, then by subject Extensive time spent maintaining indexes

Geographic filing arrangements. What if an organization conducts business in different regions of the country or the world? Might it be logical to establish files that correspond to these regions? Indeed, some businesses do employ **geographic filing** systems in which records are arranged alphabetically according to the location the records represent. Sales companies and mail-order companies are examples of companies that use geographic filing.

Questions?

What kinds of companies might use geographic filing?

How is geographic filing organized? In a geographic arrangement for the United States, the primary guide is the state, with subdivisions for the cities and counties. Records are then filed by the company name behind the proper city or county subdivision (see Figure 4-7). On the other hand, a company doing business internationally would use the country as the primary guide, with subdivisions for regions, provinces, or cities. Important records can then be filed alphabetically by company name within the appropriate subdivision.

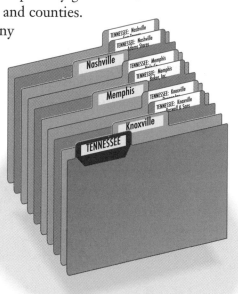

Figure 4-7 Files Arranged by Geographic Region

Table 4-6 Geographic Filing Arrangements

GEOGRAPHIC FILING	
Advantages	**Disadvantages**
Easy to locate information about particular area	Must check alphabetic index for geographic name before filing Complex system to learn More time consuming; requires double sort

Alphabetic Card Records

Questions?

What is a simple way to share information that requires repeated access?

What about the information to which an organization needs to refer frequently throughout the day? Is there a simple way to manage that type of information? The answer is yes. **Alphabetic card records** are a simple way to store information when fast, repeated access is required. For example, most organizations store the names, addresses, and telephone numbers of people and companies in alphabetic order on cards contained in file boxes or on a rotary card file.

Subject, numeric, and geographic records arrangements all use alphabetic card indexes to locate the filing unit used to store records. These indexes list subject, number, or location where the record is stored in alphabetic order. The alphabetic index is consulted before each item is filed, to determine where the file should be placed and to code the record with the proper filing unit name. This procedure is followed whether a record is stored in subject, numeric, or geographic filing arrangements. All alphabetic cards should follow the same format to ensure uniformity (see Figure 4-8).

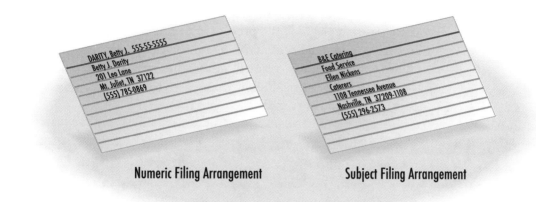

Numeric Filing Arrangement   Subject Filing Arrangement

Figure 4-8 Alphabetic Card Records

📄 What Happens When You Cannot Find It?

Misfiling is a serious problem in records management. Millions of records are lost by businesses that may never be found. There are several steps to follow when looking for a lost record or file:

1. Search through the file folder to see if the record is paperclipped to another record or is in out-of-date order in the folder.
2. Look in the folders in front of and behind the folder of the missing record.
3. Search between the folders in front and behind the folder of the missing record; the filer may have missed placing the document in the file folder and it can be wedged between the folders.
4. Look in file folders with similar name spelling.
5. Search through the offices of employees who had access to the records.
6. Check the pending file to see if the record is being held for further action.
7. If the folder is missing, scan through the entire section of the alphabetic order to see if it is misfiled.

If the record or file cannot be found after searching, you should make a new folder starting with a notation stating the date the folder was found missing. If a record is missing from the folder, you may be able to reproduce the document if it has been saved in an electronic medium.

How to Store Records

Five basic steps guide the process of preparing and storing a record in a manual system. No matter what type of manual record filing system you use, you will follow these five steps. Sometimes a sixth step is necessary. Follow these steps to ensure accurate storage of manual records.

 Storage Tips

1. Check for an individual folder behind the proper guide. If none is found, store the record in the general folder at the end of the section.
2. When placing a document in a folder, raise the folder partially rather than removing it entirely from the file cabinet. Do not pull the folder up by the tab, as this action could damage the folder's tab.
3. Verify that you have pulled the correct folder before placing the record in it.
4. Never overcrowd the folder or file drawer. Rearrange the file cabinet when necessary. Make a continuation folder if needed. Overcrowding a folder can crease or damage existing records.
5. Place the record to be filed in the front of the folder; the most recent date will be the first record in the file.
6. File records in the general folder alphabetically by name, then in chronological date order.
7. Open only one file drawer at a time. Cabinets will overbalance if more than one drawer is open, and this may result in personal injury.
8. File daily. This prevents misfiled records and makes a repetitive task easier.

Que**stions?**

What happens if a record is filed before action has been taken?

Step 1: Check to see if the record is ready to be filed. If a record is filed before action has been taken, an organization wastes time and may lose future business.

That's why it is important to **inspect** a record to make certain it is **released** for filing, determining it has been used as needed and now is ready to be put away.

A **release mark** is one way to show that the record has been used. The release mark may be a check mark, a person's initials, a line

through the document, or a symbol. Each individual in an organization may use a different release mark. Determine what mark is used by each person in your organization, and if release marks are not used, establish a release process. Document your request that individuals use release marks to communicate that a record is ready for storing. **Always look for the release mark before filing a record**.

Step 2: Determine the name of the record to be stored. How do you label records for quick retrieval? Most would agree that it is easy to determine a suitable name for alphabetic card storage, preprinted numeric storage, or internal or outgoing correspondence once you have learned the rules for **indexing** records. The difficult decision is determining the name of incoming correspondence.

Indexing is the mental process of determining the name of a record to be stored. Indexing is the most important step in storing records. Each word, letter, or symbol in the name of the record is called a **unit** of the filing segment. The first unit of the name is called the **key unit**. Individual or personal names are filed in **reverse order** with the last name as the first or key unit. Business names are filed in **as-written order** (see Table 4-7).

Table 4-7 Identifying Units by Individual or Business Name

IDENTIFYING UNITS

Individual Name			Business Name			
Kimberly	Jane	**Powers**	**Silver**	Dollar	Mining	Company
2nd unit	3rd unit	**Key unit**	**Key unit**	2nd unit	3rd unit	4th unit

Step 3: Mark the record by name for storage. Once you have determined the name of the record through indexing, the next step is to **code** the record. To do this, use a pencil to underline the main filing unit with numbers designating the following units, or write the name of the record. Never use an ink pen to code a record because it damages the record. If the record has to be photocopied at a later date, the pen markings will be visible. Pencil markings are easily erased. Coding helps an unfamiliar person know where to return a record to the correct folder.

Always look for the release mark when filing a record.

Questions? What is the most important step in storing records?

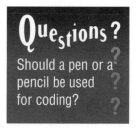

Questions? Should a pen or a pencil be used for coding?

Never use an ink pen when coding a record.

Tips for Indexing Incoming Correspondence

1. On incoming correspondence, the name on the letterhead is usually the filing unit used for storage.
2. If the stationery does not have a letterhead, the signature line can be used as the filing unit.
3. When a company name and a writer's name are of equal importance, the company name can be used as the filing unit. The writer's name may be cross-referenced.
4. Personal correspondence can be indexed by the author's name in reverse order.
5. Outgoing correspondence can be indexed by the name of the company on the inside address of the letter.
6. The subject on the reference line can be used if a special subject folder has been designated in the alphabetic filing system or in the subject filing system.
7. When there are two names of equal importance by which the record may be stored, file the record by one name and cross-reference the other name.
8. Be sure to thoroughly scan through the correspondence before determining the indexing unit.
9. If in doubt of what name by which to store the record, consult with the supervisor or manager in charge.

Step 4: Arrange the records in the order in which they will be stored in the filing system. This step, called **sorting**, saves time and energy when you actually store the records. If you do not sort the records before you are ready to store them, the fifth step will be more difficult.

There are two types of sorts. A **rough sort** may be used if the filer does not have time to physically store the record. All records are placed behind the proper alphabetic letter in a temporary holder or sorter until the filer has time to alphabetically sort and store the records. A **fine** sort is when the filer arranges all records in the proper alphabetic order before storing in the files.

Step 5: Place the records in the filing system. This step of **storing** records can be done at a time convenient to the filer. Choose a time during the day when your workload is slow, perhaps in the early morning or in late afternoon, depending on the nature of your organization's transactions. Your best bet for avoiding misfiling records is to follow the steps leading up to this one and take your time. Why be careful? Misfiling a record can be disastrous to a business. Once a record is lost, it is difficult to find.

Questions?

What time of the workday is best for filing?

Step 6: Cross-reference records. This step is not always necessary, but can help save time in the long run when there is likely to be any confusion about where a record may be stored. Cross-referencing is used for one of the following situations:

1. An individual or business changes names:

    Paulette Brown   Paulette Brown
       SEE OR   SEE
    Mrs. Gene Painter   Paulette Painter

    Denson Printing Shop
       SEE
    Fast Prints

2. The business is referred to by an acronym or an abbreviation:

    International Business Machines
       SEE
    IBM

3. There is a foreign spelling of a word or group of words:

    Republique Francaise   Bundesrepublik Deutschland
       SEE   SEE
    French Republic   Federal Republic of Germany

4. There is a compound individual name:

    Andrea Ellis-Jones
       SEE
    Andrea Jones-Ellis

5. A company has multiple names:

    Barnes, Jackson, and Potts
       SEE OR   SEE
    Jackson, Potts, and Barnes Potts, Barnes, and Jackson

6. A personal name is unusual:

    Dean James
       SEE
    James Dean

A cross-reference folder or sheet may be used to show where to look for the record. If the record is only one or two pages, a photocopy of the record can be stored in the other location instead of using a cross-reference. As with other storage methods, cross-referencing procedures help to ensure that records can be found when they're needed.

Avoid overcrowding your files with too many cross-references.

The Case of the Sluggish Filer

The local water department was awash in records. No one could understand how the correspondence to be filed was so backlogged. After some investigating, it became apparent that the culprit was not the amount of filing that had to be done, but the filer's inefficient method of filing.

The administrative assistant for the water department, Janie, was solely responsible for filing the department's records. As records accumulated on her desk, Janie would read each record, then walk over to the filing cabinets to store it. Next, she would return to her desk, scan another record, and repeat the filing procedure. What could have been accomplished in 30 minutes or less took Janie up to two hours.

Frequently, Janie would hold correspondence and other records for weeks instead of filing on a daily or weekly basis—another strategy that backfired. When the director would request a record, it would take several minutes of searching Janie's "to be filed" documents to find the requested record. It wasn't until someone pointed out a more efficient method that the problem could be corrected.

It is no wonder that Janie put off the dreaded task of filing. Just think how much easier her job would have been if she had followed the five steps of inspecting, indexing, coding, sorting, and storing. It is fortunate that the person who replaced her *did* just that.

Requests and Chargeout Procedures for Records

Chargeout programs were introduced in Chapter 3. These programs serve as guidelines for the loan and use of records. Let us explore how these programs work from a filing perspective.

To borrow a file from a centralized records center, the borrower completes a requisition request for the record or folder needed and returns the requisition to the file clerk. If the record is found, the clerk completes the **out indicator** and places it in the folder's location. An out indicator identifies the record removed, who removed the record, and the date of the loan.

There are three types of out indicators (see Figure 4-9). The out folder shows who borrowed the record and is placed in the file to replace the folder borrowed. An out slip is completed and filed in the folder when a single record or group of records are borrowed. For one or two records, it is easier to make a copy of the record, which also lessens the chance of permanently losing the borrowed record. An out guide is placed in the location of the folder that has been removed and the borrower completes the loan information on the front of the out guide.

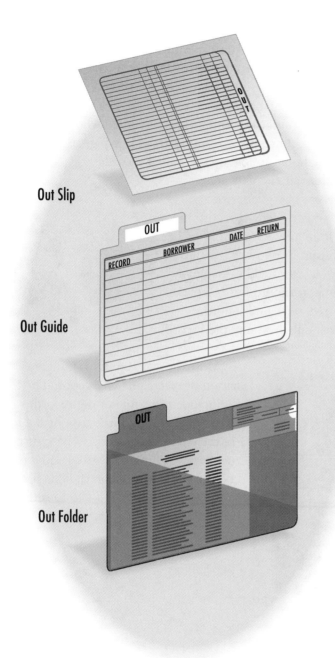

Out Slip

Out Guide

Out Folder

Figure 4-9 Elements of a Chargeout Program

If the record requested is already on loan from the records center, the borrower completes an **on-call form**. The records center and the person requesting the record each retain a copy of the on-call form. When the borrower returns the record, the clerk notifies the individual waiting to use the record.

The same chargeout procedures will apply to decentralized records. An out indicator should be completed when someone borrows a record from the filing system. The person responsible for the files should follow up on loaned records.

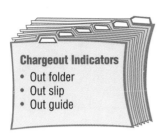

Chargeout Indicators
- Out folder
- Out slip
- Out guide

Confidential records generally have different chargeout procedures. To release a confidential record for use, a written authorization must be obtained from a company official. If the record is extremely valuable or confidential, it should not be released from the records center and the requester should examine the record on-site.

Most records centers maintain a written or electronic chargeout. The log will include the name of the record, who borrowed the record, the date of the loan, and the date the record is to be returned. The chargeout log is checked daily. If a record is not returned on the due date or before, the borrower is asked to return the record to the records center.

Storage Procedures for Filing

Inspect	Check record for the release mark before filing
Index	Determine where to store the record
Code	Mark the filing units on each record to be stored
Sort	Arrange records in the order to be stored
Store	Place each record in its proper file
Cross-reference	Document records in a secondary location to assist the search for files

Records Management in the Real World

Tracking the Misfiled Transcript

At Draughons Junior College in Nashville, all student transcripts are housed in the vault located behind the business office. When a student requests a copy of his or her transcript, the registrar and her staff are responsible for sending a copy of the transcript to the student.

There are five four-drawer filing cabinets in the vault housing approximately 500,000 transcripts. Because of the volume of records, secondary guides must be used as subdividers within each letter of the alphabet.

What happens when a transcript is misfiled? A very thorough, although not very scientific, process ensues. The registrar and her staff must think creatively—and systematically—to determine where the transcript may have "slipped through the cracks" (which is a gentle reminder to look at the bottoms of file drawers occasionally, since records have a way of finding their way there). Here is what the registrar might do to track down a missing transcript:

1. First, she searches all records within the subdivision guide. If the record is not found, a further search of the alphabetic letter is conducted.
2. The registrar will check to see if the student's transcript was filed by the first name instead of the last name or by another spelling of the last name.
3. A cross-reference alphabetic index will be checked to see if the student attended under another last name and forgot to furnish the corrected information.
4. Next, the registrar will check with the academics and admissions departments to see if the transcript was taken from the filing system without being properly charged out.
5. If the search of the other departments does not produce the needed transcript, then the registrar and her staff will begin at the beginning of the alphabet and go through the entire filing system until the transcript is found.

6. If the transcript is completely misplaced, a new transcript will be reconstructed. All grade information is stored on optical disk and organized by instructor. The business office staff will search through each semester's grades until all the student's course grades are found, and then key a new transcript.

This process can take many hours to complete and keeps staff away from other job duties, yet it is necessary to provide students with transcript documentation. For these reasons and many more, the people in the transcript area do their best to file records correctly.

KEY POINTS

For better understanding, review and reflect on the key points of this chapter.

There are six manual filing arrangements: alphabetic, numeric, alphanumeric, subject, geographic, and chronological. The type of manual filing arrangement selected should be determined by how the organization needs to access the information.

Alphabetic filing arrangements are the easiest to understand and use. Records are filed according to the letter of the alphabet.

Numeric filing arrangements assign numbers and are filed in number sequence. An alphabetic index may accompany this type of file.

Chronological files arrange records in date order. There are three types of chronological arrangements: tickler files, pending files, and reading files.

Alphanumeric filing arrangements are similar to an outline. This type of arrangement uses a combination of letters and numbers. An alphabetic index helps determine how to place and retrieve files correctly within the system.

Subject filing arranges records by topics instead of individual and company names. An alphabetic index helps determine how to place and retrieve files correctly within the system.

Geographic filing arranges records by location in alphabetic order. This type of file makes sense when an organization's activities are differentiated by region.

Alphabetic card records are used to store information that is frequently referenced. Names, addresses, and telephone numbers of persons and companies are kept on cards and stored in file boxes and in rotary systems. Subject, geographic, numeric, and alphanumeric filing systems use card indexes to locate the filing unit used to store records.

The five steps for storing records are inspecting, indexing, coding, sorting, and storing. A sixth step, cross-referencing, is used only when records can be stored by more than one name. Indexing is the most important step in storing records.

Chargeout procedures help to ensure the return of loaned documents. Chargeout procedures must be established for all records removed from their stored location.

Lost and misfiled records cost businesses millions of dollars. Searching for the record may produce the lost record. The best defense is to establish a sound filing procedure and file carefully.

True or False?
Rewrite each false item to make it a true statement.

1. All manual filing systems have different procedures, equipment, and supplies.

2. Alphabetic and chronological filing arrangements are the simplest manual filing systems.

3. All records in alphabetic filing arrangements are filed in dictionary order from A to Z.

4. The general folder will be the first folder behind the letter guide in alphabetic filing arrangements.

5. Make an individual folder for correspondence in the general alphabetic letter folder when there are six pieces of correspondence on a particular person, company, or subject.

6. Numeric, subject, and geographic filing arrangements must use an alphabetic index for storage and retrieval purposes.

7. Numeric filing arrangements assign numbers to records for storage purposes.

8. Chronological filing arrangements serve as a memory helper.

9. Subject filing arrangements use either dictionary or encyclopedic order for storage of records by topics or categories.

10. The steps for storing records will vary depending on which manual arrangement you are using.

11. A record should be inspected for a release mark before continuing the storage process.

12. Coding a record is the most important step in storing records.

13. Cross-referencing shows a second location where a record may be located within the filing system.

14. A chargeout program should be established for the loan and use of all records.

15. Confidential records borrowed from the records center should be returned to the records center before the end of the working day.

MEMORY FILE

Multiple Choice
Choose the best answer from those provided.

1. The last folder behind the alphabetic guides is called a: a) miscellaneous folder; b) mixed folder; c) general folder; d) comprehensive folder.

2. You should make an individual folder when there are ____ pieces of correspondence on a particular person, company, or subject: a) five; b) six; c) seven; d) eight.

3. This filing arrangement puts records in date order according to the day the record is to be used: a) subject; b) geographic; c) alphanumeric; d) chronological.

4. Records filed by employee number or social security number are examples of: a) numeric filing arrangements; b) alphabetic filing arrangements; c) chronological filing arrangements; d) alphanumeric filing arrangements.

5. This chronological filing arrangement acts as a temporary checklist for items currently being processed: a) tickler file; b) pending file; c) reading file; d) holding file.

6. This filing arrangement is similar to an outline; it uses a combination of letters and numbers. It is called a/an: a) numeric filing arrangement; b) chronological filing arrangement; c) alphabetic filing arrangement; d) alphanumeric filing arrangement.

7. The subject filing arrangement order that arranges records by a main topic with subdivisions filed alphabetically behind the first letter of the main topic is called: a) dictionary order; b) outline order; c) encyclopedic order; d) table of contents order.

8. Sales companies and mail-order companies are examples of companies that use this filing arrangement: a) alphabetic; b) numeric; c) subject; d) geographic.

9. The five basic steps involved in preparing and storing records are: a) indexing, coding, filing, storing , cross-referencing; b) inspecting, coding, sorting, filing, storing; c) inspecting, indexing, coding, filing, cross-referencing; d) inspecting, indexing, coding, sorting, storing.

10. This step is the most important step of the storage procedure: a) inspecting; b) indexing; c) coding; d) storing.

11. The sixth step that is sometimes needed in storing records when records may be located in two places is called: a) cross-referencing; b) cross-connecting; c) repositioning; d) relocating.

12. The guidelines established for the loan and use of records by an organization is called: a) lending library; b) chargeout program; c) loaning program; d) credit procedure.

13. When a folder is removed from its location in the records center, this item will be completed by the borrower and placed in the folder's location: a) out pointer; b) loan notice; c) borrower's symbol; d) out indicator.

14. This written or electronic document keeps track of all records borrowed from the records center and should be checked daily: a) chargeout log; b) sign-in sheet; c) account book; d) record book.

15. The maximum time a confidential record or folder is allowed to remain out of its original filing location is: a) overnight; b) 48 hours; c) the end of the working day; d) one week.

Terms to Know

Write definitions of these terms to increase your knowledge of the records management field.

alphabetic card record
alphabetic filing arrangement
alphanumeric filing
   arrangement
as-written order
chargeout program
chronological filing
   arrangement
code
cross-reference

dictionary arrangement
encyclopedic arrangement
fine sort
general record folder
geographic filing arrangement
index
inspect
key unit
misfiled record
numeric filing arrangement
on-call form
out indicator

pending file
reading file
release mark
reverse order
rough sort
sort
storing
subject filing
   arrangement
suspense file
tickler file

Make a Connection

Write or discuss your response to each question.

1. List and define the six types of manual filing systems. Give an example of each system.
2. What is the difference between dictionary and encyclopedic subject filing systems?
3. There are three types of chronological filing systems. Explain each system.
4. What are the purposes of alphabetic card systems? Which filing systems must have an alphabetic card index?
5. What are the five steps for storing records?
6. Why is the release mark important?
7. Why is indexing the most important step in storing records?
8. Why is it important to follow good sorting and storing procedures?
9. What is the sixth step for storing records? When is it used?
10. Why is a chargeout program an important control procedure to implement?
11. What steps should you take to locate a misfiled record?

The following activities require a computer and Internet connectivity.

1. Visit a search engine and see what you can find on the different types of filing systems you have studied in this chapter. What new information have you gathered that offers insights into the discussion in the text?

2. Take an online tour of the Encarta encyclopedia, published by Microsoft Corporation. How is the information arranged? Give several examples of how information is categorized.

3. Find an example of a Web site that organizes information online using characteristics of the six manual filing systems. Would you choose the same systems for the same purposes? Discuss how you would apply the system types, and explain your reasons.

4. Visit an office supply store online to review the types of chargeout supplies available. What types of supplies would you select if you were setting up a chargeout program? Why?

Thinking It Through

Dig deeper to apply what you have learned.

1. You have been hired to replace the administrative assistant at WSMT radio station. On your first day, you discover that the office is in total chaos; there is no organization of records except a few employee folders. There are no advertising account folders, and accounts have not been billed once in the past three months. The radio station should be billing the advertising customers monthly for their airtime. You discover most of this information in the assistant's desk drawer. You also find the radio station's bills stuffed in a desk drawer with no documentation showing whether or not the bills had been paid.

    While you are not pleased that the station is in such poor shape from a records management perspective, you also recognize a golden opportunity when you see it. You can prove your value to the company by helping the radio station get its records in order. Before you roll up your shirtsleeves to begin organizing customer records for billing and informational purposes, as well as developing an accounts payable filing system for the radio station's bills, you decide you need a plan. Use the following questions to guide your plan of action:

    a) How would you begin to organize the radio station's records?
    b) What type of filing systems would you use?
    c) What other types of records might be found that you would need to organize?
    d) Would a manual system be sufficient for this office?
    e) If you feel an electronic system would be helpful in meeting the needs of the radio station, how would you convince management to install an electronic records system?

2. Sally has recently been hired as your assistant to help maintain records within your department. Sally has never worked in an office before being hired by your organization. The organization does not have a formal procedures manual to aid new employees. Explain how you can help Sally perform her record-keeping job duties. What information should be covered before Sally can be allowed to handle any records?

Storage Solutions for Manual Records Systems

Tools and Equipment for Greater Efficiency

5

What's stored in this chapter?
Read on to learn...

- How to evaluate the supplies and storage equipment necessary for a filing system

- How to implement a color-coded filing system

- The importance of carefully selected manual filing equipment

- The range of equipment and tools available for manual filing systems

Questions?

? ? ? ?

Is there a wide choice of equipment for manual records storage?

Day in, day out, records accumulate. Those that are judged important enough are placed in some type of storage that permits easy access for efficient retrieval of important documents. Storage equipment and supplies for manual records come in several varieties. The specific style and type of equipment an organization chooses for manual records storage will depend on a number of factors, ranging from available space to available budget. In this chapter you will learn about options for housing records to provide convenient access to information—a vital component of a well-run office.

Equipment

Many types of equipment are used in records systems. Each individual organization will evaluate its needs before selecting the equipment to house its filing system. As you learned in Chapter 3, it is important to consider carefully the volume of records that will be stored and the longevity of the records before investing in a particular system. The following factors should be considered in the selection process:

1. **Size of the system.** Before a system is purchased for an organization, decision makers need to consider how many records require storage and estimate the projected growth of the organization, which could result in additional record storage needs. A company slated for rapid growth may require a system that is easily expandable or modifiable, while a more stable, established business may not have that requirement.

2. **Number of people accessing the system.** A system that must be accessible to more people may need different features than one that will be used exclusively by a single individual. For example, a filing system attached to an individual's workstation may be most efficient if only that person needs access. If the entire company needs access to the files, this set-up would be disruptive to work flow.

3. **Initial set-up costs.** Cost should be considered in a purchase decision, but it should not be the determining factor. The right equipment is an investment that can provide long-term benefits to the organization through business efficiency.

4. **Operating costs.** Different systems may incur a range of ongoing operating costs. Again, costs may be weighed against potential for gain through quality or improved outcomes.

Equipment Considerations
- Size of system
- Number of people
- Set-up costs
- Operating costs
- Floor space
- Security

5. **Floor space.** Available floor space may limit choices to systems that rise vertically. In addition, various equipment designs may contribute to the overall office layout and serve as room dividers to create individual workspaces.

6. **Security requirements.** If security is a concern, options may be limited to those that provide a locking system or some other provision for limiting access.

Organizations should reevaluate their records system as business needs change, considering how much storage space they require for inactive and archive records. Organizations that do not have the available space on-site may decide to store records off-site at an auxiliary location or at a record storage center. At some point in time, an organization may decide to transfer older records to micrographic or optical disk systems, which will be explained more fully in Chapter's 9 and 10.

Vertical cabinets. Vertical cabinets are the most common type of records storage equipment (see Figure 5-1). These metal cabinets hold from two to five drawers and are available in letter or legal sizes. They are also available with drawers sized for card systems. Each drawer within a vertical cabinet contains a **compressor** or **follower block** to hold the folders upright.

Figure 5-1 Vertical Cabinets

Questions?

What kind of
cabinet uses the
most floor space
relative to size?

Vertical cabinets use the most floor space relative to their size. A minimum 44-inch aisle in front of the cabinet is necessary to permit each drawer to be pulled out for proper usage. The five-drawer cabinet is the most economical because it takes up the same floor space as a two- or four-drawer cabinet.

Vertical cabinets are used for filing correspondence in alphabetic, subject, geographic, and numeric systems. They are not recommended for terminal or middle-digit numeric systems and alphanumeric systems.

Only one person can retrieve files at any time when using vertical cabinets. This can create access problems when more than one person is retrieving files from the cabinet. When controlled access is important, however, vertical cabinets work well because they are enclosed and can be locked. If fire protection is required, cabinets constructed with insulation can be purchased.

Traditional filing cabinets are constructed of steel; however, manufacturers also offer less costly units constructed of corrugated cardboard, fiberboard, or plastic.

Lateral cabinets. Lateral cabinets, available in letter and legal sizes, are a popular choice (see Figure 5-2). They are suited for long, narrow spaces where floor space is limited. Because lateral cabinets are accessed horizontally (from the side), they require only a minimum 30-inch aisle space in comparison to the 44-inch aisle space required by a vertical cabinet.

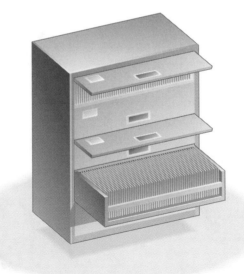

Figure 5-2 Lateral Cabinet

Lateral cabinets cost more per filing inch than vertical or shelf filing systems. Many lateral cabinets do not have follower blocks and require the use of **hanging** or **suspension files**. Suspension files add an additional cost to the filing system.

Open shelving. An open-shelf filing system stores records horizontally on shelves instead of in enclosed cabinets (see Figure 5-3). The folders are arranged in rows, with the tabs on the sides for easy reading and retrieval. Open shelves are the most economical of all filing solutions because they require 50% less floor space than alternatives and allow multiple user access.

A disadvantage of open-shelf files is that they do not provide protection to the folders from unauthorized access, fire, and water damage. Shelf filing is used for storing books and catalogs, frequently by many physicians' offices and hospitals. Color-coded systems work best in open-shelf filing.

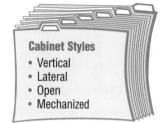

Figure 5-3 Open Shelving

Mechanized shelves. Mechanized shelves are different from conventional filing equipment because they are automated. The operator retrieves the files mechanically rather than manually. The shelves, which can be vertical or horizontal, are housed in large enclosed units with selector buttons for retrieval (see Figure 5-4). The records are stored in card, letter, or legal trays on tracks.

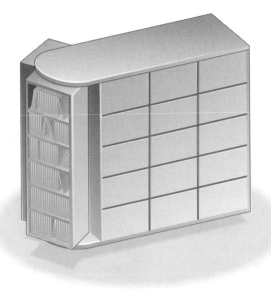

Figure 5-4 Horizontal Mechanized Shelves

Mechanized shelves are more expensive than nonmechanized equipment and should be carefully evaluated before being recommended. The weight of the equipment and the amount of floor space required must be considered in the decision. Typically, only firms using large centralized storage systems, such as insurance companies and hospitals, would require mechanized shelves.

Tools for Manual Filing
- Guides
- Folders
- Tabs
- Labels

Tools for Manual Filing Systems

The basic tools for manual filing systems are supplies used in the filing process that make it possible to organize records systematically. These tools include **guides**, **folders**, **tabs**, and **labels**. Alphabetic indexes are also be used in subject, geographic, numeric, and alphanumeric storage systems.

Guides. Visualize opening a filing cabinet drawer with 300 file folders and trying to locate a particular folder. Without guides, it takes a long time to locate the folder you are seeking. Guides are the dividers used in all storage systems to separate each alphabetic letter, subject, location, or group of numbers (see Figure 5-5).

Questions?
What are the advantages of using guides?

They serve as a street sign; they tell you where to locate the proper folder without a time-consuming search. Guides are also sturdy supports that hold folders upright in the file drawer and help prevent wear to the folder tabs when locating a particular folder. Guides are made from pressboard or filler and feature tabs for identifying the indexing unit. **Primary** guides are the main divisions in the filing system (A, B, C, D, and so on). **Secondary** guides are subdivisions of the primary guides (Ab, Ad, Al) for large filing systems.

Que**stions**?
What is the value of secondary guides?

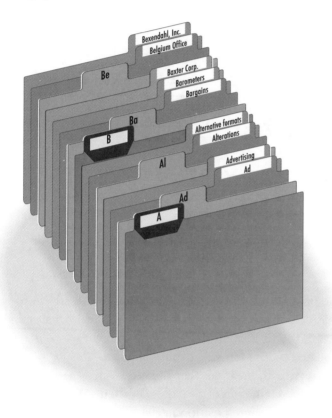

Figure 5-5 Primary and Secondary Guides

Tabs. Tabs are projections on the top edge or side of a folder or guide that extend above the regular height or width of the folder or guide. Tabs provide space for a label or caption. They can be purchased blank or preprinted with the indexing unit.

Questions?

Where would side tabs be used?

Tabs may be reinforced with metal or plastic. The tab is located on the top of the folder or guide for vertical and lateral filing cabinets. Side tabs are used for open-shelf and automated shelf filing.

Tabs come in a variety of **cuts** or extension sizes. A **straight-cut** extends the length or width of the folder. A **third-cut** extends one-third the length or width of the folder. A **fourth-cut** or **fifth-cut** may also be used (see Figure 5-6).

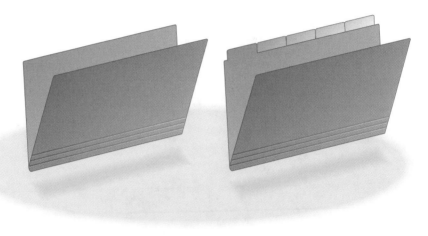

Figure 5-6 Tabs: Straight-Cut and Fifth-Cut

Questions?

What is the difference between straight-line and staggered-line positions?

The **position** of the tab is the location of the tab on the top edge or side edge of the folder. In the fifth-cut format, tabs may range from the **first position,** meaning that the tab is located on the left side of the folder, to the **fifth position,** meaning that the tab is located on the right side of the folder. When all tabs are in the same position in the filing arrangement, it is called a **straight-line** position. A **staggered-line position** means the tabs range from first to fifth position in the filing arrangement (see Figure 5-7).

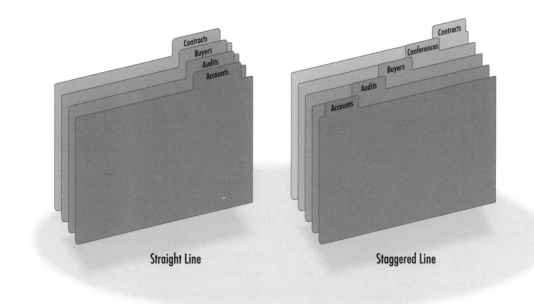

Figure 5-7 Tabs in Straight-Line and Staggered-Line Positions

Folders. Folders are the storage containers for individual records. They are made of heavy paper or plastic, and come in an assortment of colors. Folders are divided into half, with the back edge extended for the tab. The tab extension may be reinforced because this area of the folder receives the greatest use.

The base of the folder has **ridges** or **scores** that allow for folder expansion. **Scoring** is the process of manually creasing the manufacturer's ridges on the base of the folder. Scoring prevents overcrowding of the folder and reduces the possibility of the folder sliding under another folder (see Figure 5-8). The average folder holds approximately 75 sheets of paper after it is scored. All folders should be scored before using, to optimize expansion of the folder's contents. When a file folder is full, an additional folder should be started. Label the new folder identically to the original folder, but also provide the date the new folder was originated beneath the other label information.

Questions?

How does scoring improve the usefulness of a folder?

The average folder holds approximately 75 sheets of paper after it is scored.

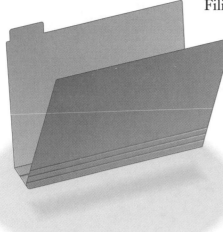

Filing cabinets without follower blocks or compressors, devices used to hold the folders pressed together in the drawer in an upright position, use hanging folders. Hanging or suspension folders have built-in hooks that allow the folder to hang from the parallel bars of the filing cabinet or a desk drawer (see Figure 5-9).

Hanging folders are more expensive than nonhanging folders. They are used for filing bulky forms such as computer printouts. Do not use suspension folders in filing cabinets containing follower blocks because they occupy approximately one-third more of the drawer space when filled and waste the storage space available for folders.

Figure 5-8 Scores along the base of a folder allow for folder expansion.

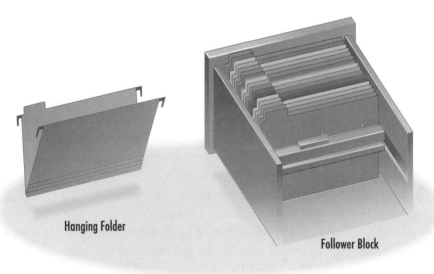

Hanging Folder

Follower Block

Figure 5-9 Hanging or Suspension Folder and Follower Block or Compressor

Labels. Labels provide a surface on which to identify the contents of each folder. They may have an adhesive backing or may be of lightweight cardboard that can be inserted into plastic holders. Labels come in a variety of sizes and colors. Color and color-striped labels make it easier to identify misfiled folders.

Uniformity in typing labels is important. All file labels should look identical when the filing cabinet is open. Depending upon the type of filing system selected, a completed label will contain a combination of letters, words, or numbers.

Rules for Typing Labels

- Always type, rather than write, a label.
- Typing on each label should begin at the same position from the top (one line down from top edge) and from the left side (in two or three spaces).
- Type personal name labels in **indexing order** (reverse order).

  Bell, James R Jr.
  Bell, James R Sr.
  Brown, Darlene M

- Type business name captions in **as-written order** (straight order).

  John Merriweather Co.
  Merry Christmas Shop
  Merry Maids Inc.

- On a straight-cut tab, the label should be affixed in the same location on all folders.
- Apply only one label per folder. If the name of the folder changes, place a new label on top of the old label.

Color-coded filing systems. Color-coded filing systems are used in most dentists' and physicians' offices and are becoming increasingly popular in all types of organizations. Color coding can save up to 50% of filing and retrieval time and reduce misfiling by up to 50% because patterns of color are easier to recognize than letters and numbers. The eye initially searches by color; when the correct color is found, a detailed search of that color yields the proper folder.

Color coding uses different colors to establish an indexing order. Colored file folders may be used to identify different departments, functions, or dates. Different years can be distinguished by using different colors for each year's records. An organization could use different colors for each department within the organization: for example, personnel—blue, engineering—red, accounting—yellow, maintenance—green, and so on.

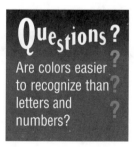

Questions?

Are colors easier to recognize than letters and numbers?

Alphabetic, numeric, and alphanumeric systems are the three main filing systems that can use color coding, as described in Table 5-1.

Table 5-1 Color Coding within Manual Filing Systems

COLOR CODING

Alphabetic	Numeric	Alphanumeric
• The first and second letters of the surname are color coded. • Each letter is assigned a different color and is imprinted on the color band. • Between 9 and 13 colors are used (varied by vendor), so the colors will be repeated.	• Ten colors are used for the numbers 0 to 10. are color coded.	• Letters are assigned a numeric value and both the letter and number

Sorters. A sorter is a temporary holder for records to be filed at a later time. Sorters may be labeled with letters or numbers preprinted on the tabs or a metal bar. Records are placed behind the proper letter or number in the proper alphabetic or numeric order until they are sorted for permanent storage.

Nonstandard Equipment

Some businesses generate large quantities of records that do not conform to conventional sizes. These records include card systems, published materials, accounting records, legal records, and engineering and architectural records. Several types of equipment are used to store these kinds of nonstandard records.

Card systems. Card systems are used for storing information with large-volume usage. Index card records are used for storing frequently used information such as names, addresses, and telephone numbers of customers, clients, suppliers, and vendors. Card records are also used to help locate the subject, geographic location, number, or alphanumeric location of a record within a conventional filing system.

There are two filing methods for card systems (see Figure 5-10). The **vertical card file** stores records upright in trays, drawers, boxes, or rotary and wheel files. Alphabetic guides are used to divide the cards. Card dimensions are usually 3 x 5", 4 x 6", or 5 x 8".

The **visible card file** stores the cards horizontally on flat trays. The description of the card is visible when the tray is open. The cards overlap, yet the bottom edge remains visible. Retrieval is faster with the visible card layout than a vertical card arrangement.

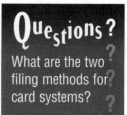

Que**stions**?

What are the two filing methods for card systems?

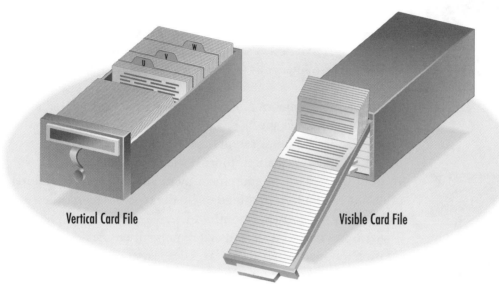

Vertical Card File   Visible Card File

Figure 5-10 Vertical and Visible Card Files

Published materials. This category of nonstandard materials includes over- or under-sized books and catalogs. Published materials are generally stored on open shelves or bookcases. Some organizations maintain extensive libraries.

Que**stions**?

How should books be indexed?

Books should be indexed by subject, author, and title, and filed by the number assigned by the indexing system. The most common indexing systems are the Dewey Decimal System and the Library of Congress System. The Dewey Decimal System features ten general divisions with ten subdivisions under each general division. The Library of Congress System is an alphabetical system of storage by subject matter.

Catalogs are filed by the name of the issuing company, with a cross-reference to the subject. Most catalog supplements are too small to file alone and should be filed in a folder next to the catalog they accompany.

Accounting records. Checks and vouchers are the most common accounting records of nonstandard size. Checks are stored in numeric order in vertical card filing systems for easy retrieval. Vouchers (sales tickets) are preprinted documents, generally larger than checks but smaller than letter-size documents, that are used by businesses to confirm that a transaction has occurred. Vouchers can be stored numerically or alphabetized by personal or company name.

Financial statements and balance sheets can be prepared either manually on journal sheets or by computerized accounting programs. Both systems require storage for a prolonged time period by the organization. Journal sheets may be stored in vertical or lateral filing equipment by month and year. Computer printouts can be stored in binders by the type of record, the year and January - December month order.

State and federal governments require all businesses to keep tax information including payroll tax, sales tax, unemployment tax, and company and employee income tax. Each of these tax records is filed separately by month, quarter, and year.

Accounts payable invoices and bills should be kept for a minimum of three working years. Records may be kept by the month and year or by the business name. Computerized accounting systems will provide a backup copy of the accounts payable of the organization but a hard copy invoice or bill should be retained in the filing system.

Legal records. Legal records may be letter (8 ½ x 11") or legal (8 ½ x 14") size, depending on the firm or government requirements. **Project ELF** (Eliminate Legal-Size Files), a program promoting the use of letter-size paper instead of legal-size paper, has been adopted by many judicial systems in the United States. This program was started by ARMA in 1980 to reduce the costs of storing documents using legal-size cabinets, folders, and paper.

Questions?

What duration of storage is required for financial statements?

Legal records may be stored alphabetically or by case number in vertical or lateral cabinets. Records stored by case number require an alphabetical card index.

Engineering and architectural records. Engineering and architectural firms use maps and drawings that require special filing arrangements. Engineering and architectural records may be stored in one of three systems: pigeonhole shelves, map cabinets, and hanging files.

Records Requiring Nonstandard Equipment
- Card systems
- Published materials
- Accounting records
- Legal records
- Engineering records
- Architectural records

Maps are usually requested by location and so are organized geographically. Drawings are requested by project number or building name and so are organized around this information.

Inactive maps and drawings are kept in pigeonhole shelves. The map or drawing is rolled and tied together with a file tag attached to the roll. This is an inexpensive method of storage, and maps and drawings will curl permanently when this method of storage is used. Semi-active maps and drawings may be stored in flat map cabinets. The drawer is labeled by the locations of maps stored. Active maps and drawings use hanging files for quick access and efficient space usage (see Figure 5-11). The maps and drawings are attached together with a clamp and the rod is labeled by location or name.

Figure 5-11 Hanging Files

Records Management in the Real World

Willa and the Fat Files

Willa, a recent college graduate, took an administrative assistant position reporting to John, an agent for a large national insurance company. During Willa's second week on the job, John requested a client's file for a meeting. Willa searched throughout the filing system and offices but could not find the client's file.

When John returned to the office later in the day, she told him she could not locate the file. John went to a separate small filing cabinet and showed Willa where his "fat files" were located. John kept this special filing cabinet for approximately 50 of his clients whose file folders were overloaded with correspondence.

Willa had learned in her Records Management class to make a continuation folder when a file had more than 75 records. John's folders had several hundred records each.

Willa shuddered with fear at the thought of dropping one of John's overcrowded fat files and having to replace all of the records in correct order. When John went out of town on business for several days, Willa took the initiative to correct John's records problem. She reorganized John's fat files and made continuation folders. Now the fat file cabinet is empty and John's files are properly stored among the alphabetic client files.

John has been amazed at the difference in locating files and working with information that was too difficult to manage in the past. And keeping the newly organized folders in good working order takes Willa only a few minutes in comparison to the time it took John to manage the thick, bulky folders. Not only has Willa improved John's efficiency, but she has made her own job much easier. No more fat files!

For better understanding, review and reflect on the key points of this chapter.

The equipment used in records systems are vertical cabinets, lateral cabinets, open shelving, and mechanized shelving. The most common equipment used is the vertical cabinet; however, this equipment takes up more space than other available options.

All records systems use tools to organize the records systematically. The same basic tools are used in all records systems: guides, tabs, folders, and labels.

An alphabetical index is used in subject, numeric, and geographic filing systems. This index provides a cross-reference list for locating information filed in the filing system.

Folders have creases on the bottom called score marks. Scoring the folder allows for folder expansion and helps the folder stay upright.

All folder labels should be uniform in appearance. Each label should be typed and the typing should begin at the same position on all labels. Labels are typed in as-written order for business names or indexed order for individual names.

Nonstandard records are records of unconventional size or shape. Nonstandard equipment is used to store card records, accounting records, legal records, published material, and engineering and architectural records.

True or False?
Rewrite each false item to make it a true statement.

1. All organizations, large and small, will use the same equipment.
2. Centralized storage systems need more floor space than decentralized storage systems.
3. Careful planning for future expansion of records storage is important in setting up a records system.
4. Vertical filing cabinets are the most popular type of records storage equipment.
5. Open-shelf filing provides both security and safety measures for records.
6. Guides are the dividers used in storage systems to separate alphabetic letters and groups of numbers, subjects, or locations.
7. Guides can be broken into first, second, and third order.
8. Tabs provide space for a label or caption on a folder or a guide.
9. Creasing the ridges on the base of the folder is called folding.
10. An additional folder should be started after the original folder reaches approximately 75 pages.
11. Labels are used to identify the contents of a folder.
12. When typing labels for both personal and business names, type the label in as-written order.
13. Color-coded filing systems reduce misfiling because misfiled folders stand out in color-coded systems.
14. A sorter is used as a temporary holder for records to be filed at a later time.
15. Nonstandard records are records of unconventional size and shape.

Multiple Choice
Choose the best answer from those provided.

1. Vertical filing cabinets are not recommended for use in the following filing arrangements: a) subject and alphanumeric arrangements; b) alphanumeric and terminal and middle-digit numeric arrangements; c) geographic and subject arrangements; d) terminal and middle-digit numeric and geographic arrangements
2. Lateral filing cabinets are suited for long, narrow spaces because:
a) they need a 30-inch aisle space; b) they are thin; c) they look more eye-appealing than other storage cabinets; d) they are inexpensive.
3. The most economical filing equipment is: a) vertical cabinets;
b) lateral cabinets; c) open-shelves; d) mechanical shelves.

4. Mechanical shelves would be used by the following types of organizations: a) small organizations with centralized filing systems; b) large organizations with centralized filing systems; c) small organizations with decentralized filing systems; d) large organizations with decentralized filing systems.

5. The dividers used in all manual filing systems to separate alphabetic letters, subjects, numbers, or locations are called: a) maps; b) locators; c) separators; d) guides.

6. The projections on the top edge or side edge of a folder or guide that extend beyond the regular height or width of the folder or guide are called: a) markers; b) clips; c) tags; d) tabs.

7. The location of the tab on the top edge or the side edge of the folder is called the: a) position; b) place; c) point; d) space.

8. Folders with built-in hooks that allow them to hang from the parallel bars of the filing cabinet or a desk drawer are called: a) hook-up folders; b) swinging folders; c) dangling folders; d) suspension folders.

9. The device used to hold folders in the file drawer in an upright position is called a: a) compactor; b) compressor; c) wedge; d) reducer.

10. An alphabetic or numeric temporary holder for documents is called a: a) classifier; b) storer; c) sorter; d) slotter.

11. Records of unconventional size and shape are called: a) nonconforming records; b) nonstandard records; c) non-regulation records; d) non-uniform records.

12. There are two types of card systems: a) visible and vertical card files; b) vertical and horizontal card files; c) visible and upright card files; d) uniform and visible card files.

13. Some organizations maintain extensive libraries for storing published materials in bookcases or on open shelves, using either of the following indexing systems: a) Library of Congress and the Guide to Records Cataloging; b) the Dewey Decimal System and the Library of Congress; c) the Guide to Records Cataloging and the Dewey Decimal System; d) Robert's Rules of Order and the Dewey Decimal System.

14. A project started by ARMA in 1980 to save on paper and supplies costs in legal offices, which has been adopted by many judicial systems in the United States, is: a) the Paperwork Reduction Act; b) Electronic Information Act; c) ERP (Electronic Records Project); d) Project ELF (Eliminate Legal Files).

15. Engineering and architectural records are stored in one of three systems: a) hanging files, pigeonhole shelves, and open shelves; b) map cabinets, pigeonhole shelves, and vertical filing cabinets; c) hanging files, pigeonhole shelves, and map cabinets; d) lateral cabinets, open shelves, and pigeonhole shelves.

Terms to Know

Write definitions of these terms to increase your knowledge of the records management field.

compressor
cut
filing manual
folder
follower blocks
guide
hanging folder
label

lateral cabinet
mechanized shelves
nonstandard record
open-shelf filing
position
primary guide
Project ELF
score marks

scoring
secondary guide
sorter
suspension folder
vertical cabinet
vertical card file
visible card file

Make a Connection

Write or discuss your response to each question.

1. What factors are considered when selecting filing equipment?
2. Describe the four most common types of filing equipment utilized by records systems.
3. Briefly explain the tools used in all manual records storage systems.
4. Why are guides necessary for manual records storage systems?
5. What is the difference between primary guides and secondary guides?
6. Why is it necessary to score a folder?
7. When is it necessary to use suspension folders?
8. What general guidelines or rules should be followed in typing folder labels? Why is label uniformity important in a records system?
9. What are the advantages of a color-coded filing system?
10. What is nonstandardized filing equipment? Briefly describe each type of equipment introduced in the chapter.

The following activities require a computer and Internet connectivity.

1. Visit an office equipment supply store on the Internet (use key words like office supplies or filing equipment to find sites). What type of filing equipment can you purchase online? Do any of the sites offer decision-making help?

2. Use an online office equipment supply site to obtain pricing information about folders, labels, and guides to complete a four-drawer vertical filing system. List items you would purchase to set up an alphabetic filing system.

3. Search the Web for fireproof file cabinets. Compare features and pricing for these products versus non-fireproof cabinets of the same size.

4. Find two companies on the Internet that produce and sell color-coded filing systems. Compare these systems for their ease of learning and use, cost of supplies, and the locations where these supplies may be purchased. Give your reasons for selecting the color-coded system you choose.

5. Visit an office supply store online. What types of nonstandard filing equipment can you purchase online? Print out a list of the equipment you find. Compare your findings with those of others in your class.

Dig deeper to apply what you have learned.

1. A new company, Jones Brothers Farm Distributors, has hired you as the office manager. Jones Brothers employs 32 people at one store location. Your first responsibility is to set up the business office. What questions do you need to ask to determine how your filing system should be set up? Be as specific as possible.

2. How would you correctly type captions to complete labels for the following personal names? Provide the correct alphabetical sequence, from front to back: Norman Newson; Dr. Regina Nagala; Nancy H. Napier; Arthur Nelson Jr.; Arthur Nelson Sr.; Rosalind Anne Nilssen.

3. You have been hired to head the new records center at Louden, Finch, and Merritt, Attorneys at Law. The firm employs 11 attorneys, 3 law clerks, 5 paralegals, and 11 legal secretaries. Each secretary keeps the active case files for his or her attorney. You will have a single assistant to help you in the records center. You will be responsible for all of the organization's inactive case files. This law firm has been practicing for over 20 years and there are approximately 450,000 inactive files. What type of equipment would you purchase? How would you set up the filing system? Draw a diagram of the records center.

Classifying Records for a Manual System

6

Alphabetic Rules for Personal, Business, and Other Names

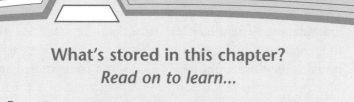

What's stored in this chapter?
Read on to learn...

- 📁 The Association of Records Managers and Administrators (ARMA) *Alphabetic Filing Rules*

- 📁 Alphabetic filing rules as they apply to personal or individual names

- 📁 Alphabetic filing rules as they apply to business names

- 📁 Alphabetic filing rules as they apply to other names (not personal or business)

- 📁 Alphabetic filing rules for filing information by subject

The ABCs—you have known them since elementary school. In addition to the alphabet's status as the foundation for our written and spoken language, it dictates the organization of many manual filing systems. Successful alphabetic filing within a manual records system requires a thorough understanding of alphabetic sequence.

It is important to follow *one* set of filing rules when storing documents alphabetically. There are several interpretations of English-language alphabetic filing. The Association of Records Managers and Administrators (ARMA) *Alphabetic Filing Rules* will be discussed in this chapter. These rules are divided into three sections: (1) personal or individual names; (2) business or company names; and (3) other names that do not fit into the personal or business groups.

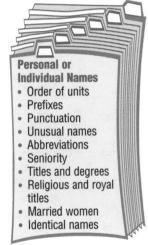

Personal or Individual Names
- Order of units
- Prefixes
- Punctuation
- Unusual names
- Abbreviations
- Seniority
- Titles and degrees
- Religious and royal titles
- Married women
- Identical names

Personal or Individual Names

Frequently a person's name is used as the **organizing unit** in an alphabetic manual filing system. The following rules govern how to sequentially place records associated with personal or individual names.

Order of units. File by name using **index** or **reverse order**. For example, the **surname** or last name is the key unit, the **given** or first name or initial is the second unit, and the middle name or initial is the third unit (Table 6-1). A unit consisting of an initial only precedes (comes before) a unit consisting of a full name.

Table 6-1 Personal Names: Order of Units

	Key Unit	2nd Unit	3rd Unit
		ORDER OF UNITS	
J. S. Cannon	Cannon	J	S
James Stephen Cannon	Cannon	James	Stephen
Joan Smith Carter	Carter	Joan	Smith
Lee Ann Carter	Carter	Lee	Ann
Leeann Carter	Carter	Leeann	

Reminder: Less before more or nothing before something when filing.

Prefixes. A **foreign article** or **particle** in a person's name is considered part of the surname (last) name. Examples include D', Da, De, Del, Della, Den, Des, El, Fitz, L', La, Las, Le, Les, Lo,

Los, M', Mac, Mc, O', Saint, San, St., Ste., Te, Ten, Ter, Van, Van de, Van Der, Von, and Von der. Disregard spacing and capitalization when indexing the key unit (Table 6-2).

Example: Ann Saint Marie is indexed as Saintmarie, Ann.

Table 6-2 Personal Names: Prefixes

PREFIXES

	Key Unit	2nd Unit	3rd Unit
Lucille M. De Bella	Debella	Lucille	M
Mike H. De Lacy	Delacy	Mike	H
Tammy B. De Marco	Demarco	Tammy	B
Cheryl Elaine La Beaux	Labeaux	Cheryl	Elaine
Elizabeth J. Le Beau	Lebeau	Elizabeth	J

Punctuation. Disregard any punctuation (hyphens, commas, periods, apostrophes) within a person's name. Consider hyphenated names as one indexing unit (Table 6-3).

Example: Luella Ferguson-Lee is indexed as Fergusonlee, Luella.

Table 6-3 Personal Names: Punctuation

PUNCTUATION

	Key Unit	2nd Unit	3rd Unit
John R. D'Amelio	Damelio	John	R
Jonathan R. D'Amelio	Damelio	Jonathan	R
Jack A. O'Brien	Obrien	Jack	A
Hugh Aaron O'Hara	Ohara	Hugh	Aaron
Linda Gail Phillips-Smith	Phillipssmith	Linda	Gail

Unusual names. Unusual names are indexed in reverse order if the surname is identifiable. If it is not possible to determine the surname, consider the last name written as the surname (Table 6-4). Cross-reference the file with the first word as the key unit.

Example: Kurt Kris is indexed as Kris, Kurt.

Table 6-4 Personal Names: Unusual Names

UNUSUAL NAMES

	Key Unit	2nd Unit	3rd Unit
Loc Nguyen	Nguyen	Loc	
	Loc	Nguyen	
	(See Nguyen Loc)		
Ping Ling Wong	Wong	Ping	Ling
	Ping	Ling	Wong
	(See Wong Ping Ling)		

Abbreviations, nicknames, and shortened names. Any **abbreviated** given names, nicknames, or brief forms of given names are considered as they are written. Do not change the spelling when indexing (Table 6-5). Nicknames can be cross-referenced if necessary.

Example: Jojo Jamison is indexed as Jamison, Jojo.

Table 6-5 Personal Names: Abbreviations, Nicknames, and Shortened Names

ABBREVIATED NAMES

	Key Unit	2nd Unit	3rd Unit
Chas. W. Foster	Foster	Chas	W
Shorty Foster	Foster	Shorty	
Billy Joe Pugh	Pugh	Billy	Joe
Wm. John Pugh	Pugh	Wm	John
Liz Robinson	Robinson	Liz	

Reminder: Place Arabic numbers before Roman numerals, numerals before words.

Seniority designations. A **seniority designation** (Jr., Sr., III) is considered the last unit (Table 6-6). File numeric designations in sequence *before* alphabetic designations. File Arabic numeric designations (1, 2, 3) before Roman numeric designations (I, II, III).

Example: John Ryan Jr. is indexed as Ryan, John Jr.

Table 6-6 Personal Names: Seniority Designations

SENIORITY NAMES

	Key Unit	2nd Unit	3rd Unit
Charles Davis III	Davis	Charles	III
Charles Davis Jr.	Davis	Charles	Jr
Charles Davis Sr.	Davis	Charles	Sr
Chas Davis Jr.	Davis	Chas	Jr
Chas Davis Sr.	Davis	Chas	Sr

Titles and degrees. All titles and degrees are the last indexing unit (Table 6-7). These include:

- Military and personal titles (e.g., Lieutenant, Reverend)
- Professional titles and educational degrees (e.g., Ph.D., M.D.)
- Professional certifications of accomplishments (e.g., CPA, CPS, RMA, CLA)

Examples: Sergeant Arnold Marchenkov is indexed as Marchenkov, Arnold Sergeant; Dr. Sally Mall is indexed as Mall, Sally Dr.; Emily Miller, CPA is indexed as Miller, Emily CPA.

Table 6-7 Personal Names: Titles and Degrees   **TITLES & DEGREES**

	Key Unit	2nd Unit	3rd Unit	4th Unit
Colonel Tom Jackson	Jackson	Tom	Colonel	
Ms. Donna Flowers, MD	Flowers	Donna	MD	Ms
Orlando Nance, CPA	Nance	Orlando	CPA	
Paulette M. Gibson, CPS	Gibson	Paulette	M	CPS
Lt. John C. Norris	Norris	John	C	Lt

Religious and royal titles. File these according to how the name is provided (Table 6-8), keeping in mind that:

- Religious and royal titles with given names only should be indexed in as-written order.
- Religious and royal titles with surnames should be indexed in reverse order.

Example: Pastor Jacob Reed is indexed as Reed, Jacob Pastor.

Table 6-8 Personal Names: Religious and Royal Titles   **RELIGIOUS/ROYAL**

	Key Unit	2nd Unit	3rd Unit
Father John	Father	John	
Sister Marie	Sister	Marie	
Father Timothy Baker	Baker	Timothy	Father
Rabbi Dennis Ruben	Ruben	Dennis	Rabbi
Sister Mary Sullivan	Sullivan	Mary	Sister

Married women. A married woman's name is indexed in reverse order. Many women use their maiden name hyphenated with their married name. The double name would be considered one unit, with the hyphen omitted. Create a cross-reference if you are aware that an alternate form of the married woman's name is used (Table 6-9).

Example: Lydia Smitty-Olson is indexed as Smittyolson, Lydia.

Table 6-9 Personal Names: Married Women

	Key Unit	2nd Unit	3rd Unit	4th Unit
Linda Bennett-Brown	Bennettbrown	Linda		
Julie Smith Fann	Fann	Julie	Smith	
Donna R. Hooper, CPA	Hooper	Donna	R	CPA
Ann Marie Reed	Reed	Ann	Marie	
See Ann Marie West	West	Ann	Marie	
Mrs. James Jones	Jones	James	Mrs	
See Janice Jones	Jones	Janice		

Identical names. If all units are identical in the names of two or more individuals, use address information to determine your sequence (Table 6-10). Consider the city first, followed by the state or province, street names, and then house or building numbers to determine the alphabetical order. ZIP codes are not considered as an indexing unit.

Example: The folder for Reynolds, Jack, who lives in Elgin, Illinois, precedes the folder for Reynolds, Jack, residing in Rutherford, Illinois.

Table 6-10 Personal Names: Identical Names

	Key Unit	2nd Unit	3rd Unit	4th Unit	5th Unit	6th Unit	7th Unit
Laura Meyer Knoxville, TN	Meyer	Laura	Knoxville	TN			
Laura Meyer Nashville, TN	Meyer	Laura	Nashville	TN			

Tonya Thomas
  101 3rd St.
  Detroit, MI
	Thomas	Tonya	Detroit	MI	3rd	St	101

Tonya Thomas
  1826 3rd St.
  Detroit, MI
	Thomas	Tonya	Detroit	MI	3rd	St	1826

Business or Company Names

Information is frequently gathered pertaining to a business or company. The name of the business or company becomes the organizing unit, for which the following rules apply.

Figure 6-1 Sample Sequence of Personal Names

Order of units. Each word in a business name is a separate indexing unit (Table 6-11).

- Units in a business name are considered as-written, including a person's name in a business name.
- If *The* is the first word in a business name, it becomes the last indexing unit.

Examples: Ron's Deli is indexed as Rons Deli; The O'Reilly Steak House is indexed as Oreilly Steak House The.

Business or Company Names
- Order of units
- Prefixes
- Prepositions, conjunctions, articles, and symbols
- Punctuation and possessives
- Single letters and abbreviations
- Titles
- Numbers
- Identical names

Table 6-11 Business Names: Order of Units

ORDER OF UNITS

	Key Unit	2nd Unit	3rd Unit	4th Unit
Closets Unlimited	Closets	Unlimited		
The Clothes Horse	Clothes	Horse	The	
Clyde's Cycles	Clydes	Cycles		
Bob Jones' Body Shop	Bob	Jones	Body	Shop

Prefixes. A foreign article or particle in a business name is part of the word it precedes. Examples include D', Da, De, Del, De La, Della, Den, Des, Di, El, L', La, Las, Le, Les, Los, M', Mac, Mc, O', Saint, San, St., Ste, Te, Ten, Ter, Van, Van De, Van Der, and Von. Disregard any spacing or capitalization when indexing the unit (Table 6-12).

Example: Van De Meter Drycleaners is indexed as Vandemeter Drycleaners.

Table 6-12 Business Names: Prefixes

PREFIXES

	Key Unit	2nd Unit	3rd Unit
La Vogue Boutique	Lavogue	Boutique	
Le Mail Boxes	Lemail	Boxes	
San Antonio Taco Stand	Sanantonio	Taco	Stand
San Diego Surfboards	Sandiego	Surfboards	
St. Paddy's Irish Pub	Stpaddys	Irish	Pub

Prepositions, conjunctions, articles, and symbols. Consider all words as separate indexing units (Table 6-13). Index symbols (e.g., &, %, $, #) as if they were spelled out (e.g., and, percent, dollar, number).

Example: Gibbon & Ross Law Offices is indexed as Gibbon and Ross Law Offices.

Table 6-13 Business Names: Prepositions, Conjunctions, Articles, and Symbols

PREPOSITIONS

	Key Unit	2nd Unit	3rd Unit	4th Unit
The 5 & 10	5	and	10	The
The #'s Game Store	Numbers	Game	Store	The
The $ Store	Dollar	Store	The	
Sense and %s	Sense	and	Percents	
+ Sizes	Plus	Sizes		

Punctuation and possessives. Disregard all punctuation in business names. Consider hyphenated words as one indexing unit (Table 6-14).

Example: World's Best Card Shop! is indexed as Worlds Best Card Shop.

Table 6-14 Business Names: Punctuation and Possessives

	Key Unit	2nd Unit	3rd Unit
A-1 Signs	A1	Signs	
A-Z Office World	AZ	Office	World
Barry's Bi-Rite	Barrys	Birite	
Design-A-Sign	Designasign		
Thomas-Jones Nursery	Thomasjones	Nursery	

PUNCTUATION

Single letters and abbreviations. Pay attention to these different filing rules (Table 6-15).

- Single letters in a business name are indexed as-written. If there are spaces between the letters, each letter is a separate indexing unit. Disregard periods and hyphens.
- **Acronyms** (words formed by taking the first letter of several words) are indexed as one unit.
- Abbreviations in business names are indexed as-written. Do not spell out the word.
- Radio and television **call letters** are indexed as one word.

Examples: P.J. Nelson Auto Parts is indexed as PJ Nelson Auto Parts; WLDY Radio Station is indexed as WLDY Radio Station.

Table 6-15 Business Names: Single Letters and Abbreviations

	Key Unit	2nd Unit	3rd Unit
GAB Business Services	GAB	Business	Services
G. D. E.	G	D	E
IBM	IBM		
Wm. Rogers Corp	Wm	Rogers	Corp
WMIX Radio Station	WMIX	Radio	Station

ABBREVIATIONS

Titles in business names. Titles in business names are indexed in as-written order (Table 6-16).

Example: Sergeant Pepper's Music Warehouse is indexed as Sergeant Peppers Music Warehouse.

Table 6-16 Business Names: Titles in Business Names

TITLES

	Key Unit	2nd Unit	3rd Unit	4th Unit
Sir Video	Sir	Video		
Sister Marie's Girls Home	Sister	Maries	Girls	Home
Capt. Bob's Seafood Feast	Capt	Bobs	Seafood	Feast
Madam Noelle's Millinery	Madam	Noelles	Millinery	
Admiral Young's Boat Dock	Admiral	Youngs	Boat	Dock

Numbers in business names. There are several rules to follow when numbers are used in the business name (Table 6-17).

- Numbers spelled out in business names are indexed as-written and arranged in alphabetic order.
- When a name with a number written as figures is the first word, the numbers are arranged in **ascending numeric order** (lowest to highest) before all alphabetical street names.
- File Arabic numeric designations (1, 2, 3) before Roman numeric designations (I, II, III).
- Names with inclusive numbers (e.g., 23–65) are arranged by the first number (e.g., 23) only.
- If numbers comprise a unit of the name other than the key unit, and all units preceding the numbers are identical, the number unit precedes units composed of the spelled-out word unit.
- If the number contains a -*st*, -*nd*, -*rd*, or -*th* ending, drop the ending and consider the number only.

Example: 24-Hour Grocery is indexed as 24Hour Grocery; 2nd Time Around Sports Gear is indexed as 2 Time Around Sports Gear.

Table 6-17 Business Names: Numbers in Business Names

	Key Unit	2nd Unit	3rd Unit	4th Unit
12 Point Motel	12	Point	Motel	
Twelve Oaks Motel	Twelve	Oaks	Motel	
4-Wheel Alignment	4Wheel	Alignment		
4th Street Café	4	Street	Cafe	
110-220 Smith Bldg	110220	Smith	Bldg	
Tina's 5 Star Grill	Tinas	5	Star	Grill
Tina's 5'4 & Under	Tinas	5Foot4	and	Under
West 32nd St Restaurant	West	32	St	Restaurant

NUMBERS

Identical names of businesses. When more than one business has the same name, use the address to determine the alphabetical order (Table 6-18). Consider the following in order: city, then the state or province, street name, and then the house or the building numbers.

Example: Berg Deli in Appleton is placed before Berg Deli in Arlington.

Table 6-18 Business Names: Identical Names of Businesses

IDENTICAL NAMES

	Key Unit	2nd Unit	3rd Unit	4th Unit	5th Unit	6th Unit	7th Unit
Triple A Florist Athens GA	Triple	A	Florist	Athens	GA		
Triple A Florist Athens TN	Triple	A	Florist	Athens	TN		
Willow Tree Nursery Bluff Road Charlotte NC	Willow	Tree	Nursery	Charlotte	NC	Bluff	Rd
Willow Tree Nursery Lansing Ave Charlotte NC	Willow	Tree	Nursery	Charlotte	NC	Lansing	Ave
Nifty Pets 450 Washington Pl Reston VA	Nifty	Pets	Reston	VA	Washington	Pl	450
Nifty Pets 2200 Washington Pl Reston VA	Nifty	Pets	Reston	VA	Washington	Pl	2200

Other Names

The Association of Records Managers and Administrators (ARMA) has established alphabetic filing rules pertaining to non-personal, nonbusiness entities.

School names. The name of the elementary school, secondary school, college, university, or special school is indexed as-written (Table 6-19). When the word *The* appears in the school name as the first word, consider it the last unit of the name for filing purposes.

Examples: Hampton Academy of Music is indexed as Hampton Academy of Music; The Newton School is indexed as Newton School The.

Table 6-19 Other Names: School Names **SCHOOL NAMES**

	Key Unit	2nd Unit	3rd Unit	4th Unit
Acklen Women's College	Acklen	Womens	College	
George Smith High School	George	Smith	High	School
Jo Allen Middle School	Jo	Allen	Middle	School
Percy Priest Academy	Percy	Priest	Academy	
Martha Mills University	Martha	Mills	University	

Religious institutions. The names of cathedrals, churches, synagogues, temples, and the like are indexed as-written (Table 6-20). In case of identical names, the city, followed by the province or state, is used to determine the alphabetical order.

Example: Prince of Peace Lutheran Church is indexed as Prince of Peace Lutheran Church.

Table 6-20 Other Names: Religious Institutions **RELIGIOUS**

	Key Unit	2nd Unit	3rd Unit	4th Unit	5th Unit
Christ Episcopal Church	Christ	Episcopal	Church		
Community Unification Church	Community	Unification	Church		
The Jewish Temple Gulfport, MS	Jewish	Temple	The	Gulfport	MS
The Jewish Temple Jackson, MS	Jewish	Temple	The	Jackson	MS
St. Henry's Catholic Church	Sthenrys	Catholic	Church		
Three Rivers Baptist Church	Three	Rivers	Baptist	Church	

Organizations and associations. The names of clubs, fraternal orders, health organizations, lodges, societies, unions, and similar groups are indexed in as-written order (Table 6-21).

Example: Rotary Club of North America is indexed as Rotary Club of North America.

Table 6-21 Other Names: Organizations and Associations

ORGANIZATIONS

	Key Unit	2nd Unit	3rd Unit	4th Unit
Al-Menah Shrine Temple	Almenah	Shrine	Temple	
Fraternal Order of Police	Fraternal	Order	of	Police
Jewish Community Center	Jewish	Community	Center	
Kappa Delta Alpha	Kappa	Delta	Alpha	
American Medical Assoc.	American	Medical	Assoc	

Financial institutions. The names of banks, trust companies, savings and loan associations, and other financial institutions are indexed as-written (Table 6-22). When the names are identical, the city, followed by province or state, is considered in determining the alphabetical order. Branch names are considered after the institution, city, province, or state names.
Example: First Federated Bank is indexed as First Federated Bank.

Table 6-22 Other Names: Financial Institutions

FINANCIAL

	Key Unit	2nd Unit	3rd Unit	4th Unit	5th Unit
National Savings & Loan	National	Savings	and	Loan	
Bank of Kansas Lincoln Branch	Bank	of	Kansas	Lincoln	Branch
Bank of Kansas Newton Branch	Bank	of	Kansas	Newton	Branch
1st Federal Trust Boston MA	1	Federal	Trust	Boston	MA
1st Federal Trust Jackson MS	1	Federal	Trust	Jackson	MS

Guardians, trustees, receivers, and agents. Guardians, trustees, receivers, and agents that act for another person or organization are not indexed. A guardian, trustee, receiver, or agent may be a person, company, or financial institution. Records are filed by the name of the person or organization for whom the guardian or agent is acting (Table 6-23). A cross-reference may be used for referencing the name of the guardian or agent.

Table 6-23 Other Names: Guardians, Trustees, Receivers, and Agents

GUARDIANS

	Key Unit	2nd Unit	3rd Unit
First National Bank Trustee for Lisa Dawson	Dawson	Lisa	
John F. York Guardian for Wm. Jeffries	Jeffries	Wm	
Elliott & Sweeney Receivers for Noel Furniture Company	Noel	Furniture	Company
Daniel J. Noel Trustee for Toni Marie Singleton	Singleton	Toni	Marie
Cross-Country Movers Agents for Flowers Van Lines	Flowers	Van	Lines

Subsidiaries and divisions. A subsidiary, division, or affiliate of a parent company is filed under their own name with a cross-reference to the parent company (Table 6-24).

Table 6-24 Other Names: Subsidiaries and Divisions

SUBSIDIARIES

	Key Unit	2nd Unit	3rd Unit
Aerostructures Corp	Aerostructures	Corp	
Gaylord Entertainment	Gaylord	Entertainment	
Kraft Foods, Inc.	Kraft	Foods	Inc
Oscar Mayer & Co.	Oscar (See also Kraft Foods, Inc.)	Mayer	Co
Textron Industries	Textron (See also Aerostructures Corp)	Industries	
Wildhorse Saloon	Wildhorse (See also Gaylord Entertainment)	Saloon	

Newspapers, periodicals, and other publications. The names of newspapers, periodicals, and other publications are indexed in as-written order (Table 6-25). If the names are identical, the city, then the province or state are used for indexing purposes.

Government names. Government names include local, state, and federal agencies as well as foreign governments. When there are many records to be stored, the best rule is to house these records alphabetically in a designated section of the filing cabinet. If these records are stored with other correspondence, use the following rules:

Table 6-25 Other Names: Periodicals and
Other Publications

PERIODICALS

	Key Unit	2nd Unit	3rd Unit	4th Unit
Planting Seasons	Planting	Seasons		
Daily Herald Gulfport MS	Daily	Herald	Gulfport	MS
Daily Herald Columbia TN	Daily	Herald	Columbia	TN
Wall Street Journal	Wall	Street	Journal	
Fashion World	Fashion	World		

1. **Federal names.** The first three units for any federal government name are *United States Government.* These words should be written on any record to which they apply. The fourth and succeeding units are the name of the office, bureau, department, and so on, as it appears on the letterhead. The words *Department of, Office of, Bureau of,* and *Division of* are transposed and used as units when they are part of the official name (Table 6-26).

Table 6-26 Other Names: Federal Government Names

GOVERNMENT

	Key Unit	2nd Unit	3rd Unit	4th Unit	5th Unit	6th Unit	7th Unit	8th Unit
Environmental Protection Agency	United	States	Government	Environmental	Protection	Agency		
Department of Justice								
Drug Enforcement Administration	United	States	Government	Justice	Dept (of)	Drug	Enforcement	Administration
Department of Justice								
Federal Bureau of Investigation	United	States	Government	Justice	Dept (of)	Federal	Bureau (of)	Investigation
Department of the Treasury								
Internal Revenue Service	United	States	Government	Treasury	Dept (of the)	Internal	Revenue	Service
Department of Labor								
Bureau of Labor Statistics	United	States	Government	Labor	Dept (of)	Labor	Statistics	Bureau (of)

2. **State, province, commonwealth, and territory names.** The key unit is the name of the state, province, commonwealth, or territory. The second unit is the state, province, commonwealth, or territory, if it is necessary to distinguish between this level and the next or lower level (city, county, township, and so on). The succeeding units are the principal words in the name of the bureau, department, board, or office. *Department of, Office of,* and so on, are the last indexing unit (Table 6-27).

STATE NAMES

	Key Unit	2nd Unit	3rd Unit	4th Unit
Florida Highway Patrol	Florida	Highway	Patrol	
Oklahoma Dept. of Education	Oklahoma	Education	Dept	of
Puerto Rico Health Dept.	Puerto	Rico	Health	Dept
Tennessee Bureau of Investigation	Tennessee	Investigation	Bureau	of
Kentucky General Services Department	Kentucky	General	Services	Department

3. **County, borough, parish, city, town, township, and village.** The key unit is the name of the county, city, town, and so on. The second unit is usually the word *County*, *Borough*, *Parish*, *City*, *Town*, *Township*, or *Village*. The succeeding units are the principal words in the name of the department, bureau, board, or office. *Department of*, *Office of*, and so on, are the last indexing unit (Table 6-28). State names are considered if all names are identical and the state name follows after the county, city, township, and so on.

Table 6-28 Other Names: County, Borough, Parish, City, Town, Township, and Village

COUNTY NAMES

	Key Unit	2nd Unit	3rd Unit	4th Unit	5th Unit	6th Unit	7th Unit
City of Murfreesboro General Sessions Court	Murfreesboro	City	of	General	Sessions	Court	
Roads Division, Public Works Department, Branson County	Branson	County	Public	Works	Department	Roads	Division
Jackson Parish Water Treatment System	Jackson	Parish	Water	Treatment	System		
City of Old Hickory Sheriff's Department	Old	Hickory	City	of	Sheriffs	Department	
Hopewell Community Center, City of Lakewood	Lakewood	City	of	Hopewell	Community	Center	

4. **Foreign government names.** The English name of the foreign country is the key unit. This is followed by the name of the office, bureau, or department, in the same manner as other government names (Table 6-29). The foreign spelling should be cross-referenced or listed in an index.

Table 6-29 Other Names: Foreign Government Names

	Key Unit	2nd Unit	3rd Unit	4th Unit
FOREIGN NAMES				
Principat d'Andora				
Principality of Andora	Andora	Principality	of	
Cote d'Ivoire				
Ivory Coast	Ivory	Coast		
Republic of Bharat				
Republic of India	India	Republic	of	
Bundesrepublik Deutschland				
Federal Republic of Germany	Germany	Federal	Republic	of
Republica Federativa do Brazil				
Federative Republic of Brazil	Brazil	Federative	Republic	of
Royaume de Belgique (french)				
Koninkrijk Belgie (dutch)				
Kingdom of Belgium	Belgium	Kingdom	of	

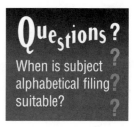

Questions?

When is subject alphabetical filing suitable?

Storage by Subject within Alphabetic Arrangement

Sometimes it is appropriate to store records within an alphabetic filing arrangement by subject title instead of personal or business names. Subject alphabetical filing is used when the subject title is more important than the personal or business name. An example would be an engineering firm participating along with other firms in special projects. Each project name, rather than the name of the various participating firms, would be more frequently requested. For easier and faster retrieval of files, a person could find all records regarding a project in one location by subject instead of searching by individual businesses assigned to the same project.

Another example would be prospective employee applications. All applications pertaining to the records manager position would be stored under Applications - Records Manager. This makes better sense than storing resumes under the applicant's surname.

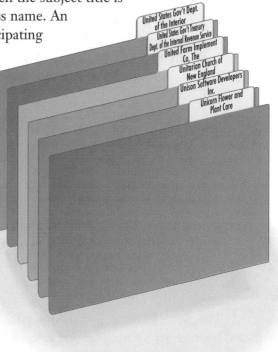

Figure 6-2 Sample Sequence of Business Names

Records Management in the Real World

Noleen Sullivan

Noleen Sullivan was the office manager for the Gowda Ear, Nose, and Throat Clinic for 26 years. When Noleen started with Dr. Gowda, the office consisted of Dr. Gowda; Bonnie, the nurse; and Noleen. Through the years, Dr. Gowda added four physicians to his practice, and the office and medical staff increased to 27 people at two office locations.

When Noleen came to work for Dr. Gowda, all patient records were filed alphabetically, A to Z, in vertical filing cabinets. He had just begun practicing medicine shortly before Noleen arrived to work with him, but she knew immediately that this system would not work for long. Dr. Gowda's practice grew rapidly and Noleen began investigating offices of doctors with larger practices in order to study their record systems.

Noleen discovered that most doctor's offices rely on color-coded alphabetical filing systems on open shelves. Noleen said that there are several reasons doctor's offices prefer to work with open-shelf filing equipment. Such a system allows for easy expansion of records as the filing systems grow. In a busy doctor's office, such as the Gowda ENT Clinic, it is much easier to pull a patient's records when the records are visible. With open shelves you have this advantage.

Learning how to use a color-coded alphabetical filing system was more difficult than mastering the straight alphabetic A to Z filing to which Noleen was accustomed. However, once she learned how to color-code the patients' records, Noleen said that the system made it easier to find the record when it was needed and to refile it when it was no longer in use.

A color-coded alphabetical filing system saves time and effort in a busy doctor's office. Most doctor's offices do not have time to search for misfiled records when a sick patient is on the telephone. Color-coded filing systems reduce misfiled records by 50%.

When the Gowda ENT Clinic established its second location, Noleen was called in to set up this location because of her expert office skills.

For better understanding, review and reflect on the key points of this chapter.

Personal names are filed in index or reverse order. Within this basic structure, various rules dictate how to determine the order of units given different characteristics of the personal name.

Business names are filed in as-written order. Specific rules guide the filing of business names given different characteristics of the business name.

Non-personal and non-business names are filed in as-written order. These include schools, religious institutions, financial institutions, and other non-business organizations.

Subject alphabetical filing is another approach to alphabetical filing. It is used when the subject title is more important than the personal or business name.

True or False?
Rewrite each false item to make it a true statement.

1. A person's name is filed in as-written order.

2. The rule is "something before nothing when filing."

3. Any punctuation within a person's name is disregarded.

4. Always spell out abbreviated names, nicknames, or brief forms of given names.

5. All titles (Sr., CPS, Dr., etc.) are the last indexing unit.

6. Royal and religious titles with given names only are indexed in as-written order.

7. Business names are filed in indexing or reverse order.

8. If The is the first word in a business name, it becomes the last indexing unit.

9. A foreign article or particle in a personal or business name is part of the word it precedes.

10. Acronyms are indexed as separate units and filed accordingly.

11. Arabic numbers are filed before Roman numerals.

12. If business names are identical, the alphabetical order is determined by the address.

13. Check the city and then the state in determining the alphabetical order in identical names.

14. The first three units for any federal government agency are United States Government.

15. Never mix any subject files within alphabetical filing arrangements; always make a separate filing drawer for these files.

Multiple Choice
Choose the best answer from those provided.

1. Which of the following personal names is out of order? a) Barrett, C J; b) Barlett, Charles J; c) Barrett, Charles J; d) Barrett, Charles James.

2. Which of the following personal names is out of order? a) Welch, Lesa D; b) Welch, S J; c) Welch, Lisa D; d) Welch, Lisa Diane.

3. Which of the following seniority designations is out sequence? a) Nance, Orlando Thomas, Jr.; b) Nance, Orlando, III; c) Nance, Orlando, IV; d) Nance, Orlando Thomas, Sr.

4. Select the personal name that is incorrectly indexed: a) Martin, John Reverend; b) Thomas, Henry Father; c) John Father; d) Jordan, Francis Brother.

5. Which of the following business names is out of order? a) a) the Print Shop; b) Pro Cuts; c) Pro-top Nails; d) Probowling Lanes.

6. Which of the following business names is out of order? a) T & S Finance; b) TCM, Inc.; c) T C L Enterprises; d) TCH Limos.

7. Which of the following business names is incorrect? a) Basantes; b) Elpalmas Mexican Restaurant; c) Kathys Bakery; d) Mama Mia's.

8. Which radio station or television station call letters are incorrect? a) WHTV; b) WMAC; c) WSMV; d) W W T N.

9. In case of identical names, what address order determines the alphabetical order? a) street, city, state; b) state, city, street; c) city, street, state; d) city, state, street.

10. Which of the following business names is out of order? a) Jones Pools, 120 Old Hickory Boulevard, Nashville, Tennessee; b) Jones Pools, 235 Highway 41, Nashville, Indiana; c) Jones Pools, 89 Louisville Pike, Nashville, Indiana; d) Jones Pools, 898 Old Hickory Boulevard, Nashville, Tennessee.

11. When indexing schools, religious institutions, organizations, and associations, and *The* is the first word in the title, what indexing unit is it? a) dropped from title; b) first; c) last; d) none of the above.

12. To determine the alphabetical order for financial institutions with identical names, the indexing order will be: a) branch, city, then state; b) city, state, then branch; c) state, city, then branch; d) none of the above.

13. Guardians, trustees, receivers, and agents act for another person or organization and these records are filed by: a) the name of the guardian, trustee, receiver, or agent; b) the person or organization they act for; c) the financial institution using them; d) none of the above.

14. The first three units in federal government agencies are: a) United States Departments; b) United States Agencies; c) United States Government; d) none of the above.

15. Foreign government names are filed with the key unit being: a) the foreign spelling; b) the English spelling of the foreign name; c) both the foreign and English spelling on the label; d) none of the above.

Terms to Know

Write definitions of these terms to increase your knowledge of the records management field.

abbreviation
acronym
as-written order
ascending order
call letters
foreign article
foreign particle

given name
index order
organizing unit
reverse order
seniority designation
surname

Make a Connection

Write or discuss your response to each question.

1. Arrange the following personal names in indexing order. Underline the key unit and mark the second, third, fourth, and succeeding units by number.

	2	**3**
Example: David T. Adams	<u>Adams</u> David	T

David T. Adamson, MD
Chris & Brandy Bailey
Bradford Alan Bishop, CPA
J. A. Blaine
Eldon Easton Blake
Mr. Albert Blakely, Sr.
David Childress, Attorney
David A. Childress
J. Don Dunaway
Will H. Gilbert, USN

Rev. W. R. Hazelwood
Father Timothy
Barbara Gail Kennedy, CPS
Greg and Jan Lewis
Newton Mac Leod, Sr.
Thomas C. Meadows
Osamu Nakachi
Chas W. Parrish
Mimi Neely-Jones
H. Philip Nabors

Make a Connection

2. Arrange the following business names in indexing order. Underline the key unit and mark the second, third, fourth, and succeeding units by number.

		2	**3**
Example: The Mad Hatter		<u>Mad</u> Hatter	The

2 Men and a Truck	Aunt Mary's Hair Salon
G & H Alarms	All-My-Sons Moving & Storage
Rosie's Carpet Cleaning	R S Wallace Masonry
A 24 Door Repair	J. T. Dugger & Sons
All-City Appliances	Sister Ann's Coffee House
A+ Fence Co.	E-Z Mortgage Co.
Frugal Fabrics	La Bistro
Colonel Bob's Glass Act	JLM Office Products
Molly Maids	Joe's Chimney Sweeps
The Barn Yard	Flower Power Garden Center

3. Arrange the following other names in indexing order. Underline the key unit and mark the second, third, fourth, and succeeding units by number.

Example: United States Government Social Security Administration Office of Hearings and Appeals

     2   **3**   **4**   **5**   **6**   **7**   **8**   **9**

<u>United</u> States Government Social Security Administration Hearings and Appeals

10 11

Office of

    Atlanta Codes Adminstration Building Plans Review Division
    Charlotte Courts System Criminal Division Court Clerk Office
    Lexington Department of Education Magnet School Program

Make a Connection

Phoenix Parks & Recreation Department Sports & Athletics Division
Shelby County Police Department DARE Program
Louisiana Wildlife Resources Agency Fish Management Services
Tennessee Department of the Military Emergency Management Agency
Tennessee Department of Revenue Tax Enforcement Administration
Vermont Human Services Department Family Assistance Division
United States Government Department of Agriculture Farm Service Agency
United States Government Department of Commerce Census Bureau
United States Government Department of Defense Marine Corps Recruiting
     Station
United States Government Internal Revenue Service Minneapolis Office
United States Government Treasury Department Secret Service Bureau Law
     Enforcement Office

4. Arrange the following personal names in alphabetic order.

Brian Michael	Chas R. Beasley
John M. Abernathy, Jr.	Robbie L. Kennedy
John Abernathy, III	John M. Abernathy, III
Danny C. Duke	Danay C. Duke
Judith Ann Biggs	Robert L. Kennedy
Sister Anna Marie	Dwight D. Nash
Charles L. Beasley	Daniel C. Duke
Franklin J. La Mar	
Judy Ann Biggerstaff	Julie Brown-Lee
Steven Michaels	

A. L. Anderson   376 Clearlake Dr.   Memphis, TN
A. L. Anderson   934 Drummond Dr.   Memphis, TN

Make a Connection

5. Arrange the following business names in alphabetic order.

U-Haul It, Inc.	Mrs. Clean Housekeeping
G E C	B-Dry, Inc.
Lain's Tree Surgery	Nashville Billiard Store
Anti-Pest Exterminators	The Mulch Man
The Pink House	BFK Contractors
Mr. T's Patio Furniture	Patricia Ann's Tabletops & Gifts
ABC Gutters	Chris-Moore, Inc.
Wizard of DOS	The Mad Platter
Hart/Freeman Architects	Larry Ball Designs
A-1 Lock Services	AAA Wallpaper & Floors

6. Arrange the following other names in alphabetic order.

Department of Justice Bureau of Prisons

St. Louis City Agricultural Extension Services 4-H Club

Florida Department of the Military Army National Guard

New York City Police Department Theft Unit

Department of Labor Wage & Hour Division Nashville District Office

St. Paul Dental Clinic Department of Health

Tennessee Department of Commerce & Insurance Consumer Affairs Division

Utah Department of Health Vital Statistics Division

United States Government Tennessee Valley Authority Office of Inspector General

City of Memphis Assessor of Property Property Records Division

Georgia Human Services Department Child Care Licensing

United States Government Postal Services Administrative Offices

Department of Defense Department of Navy NROTC Unit

Washington State Department of Revenue Audit Division

Nashville & Davidson County Election Commission Voter Registration

Make a Connection

7. Arrange the following combination names in alphabetic order.

Liberty National Savings & Loan	Pat's Taxidermy
Charles David Chitwood	ABC Fence Company
Tiny Tots Daycare	J.O. Baggett
Fall Creek Roadside Market	T. Roy Adams
The Children's Learning Tree	Art the Painter
Nancy Jones-Kennedy	1st Global Finance Corp.
You Store It	Off the Tee Driving Range
Diana Van Winkle	Buford Hiles III
WWAK AM/FM	Buford Hiles Jr.
Wash-N-Go Car Wash	Billy Bob's Dancing Hall
Woodbury Elementary School	Fix-a-Dent Collision Center
S and H Express Line	Paula Ann Lawson
Dr. Robert Shelley	Samuel V. Lazenby, MD
Spring Hill Garden and Nursery	City of Mt. Juliet Public Works
Timothy M. Le Grand	Department
Osborne Watch Repair	Native Healing Techniques
Custom Shower Doors & Mirrors	Nestor & Sons, Inc.
Lisa A. Shouse	Old Hickory Country Club
Wiley Electrical Equipment Suppliers	All Night Long Electric Co.
Pet Doc	W. Douglas Vaughn
Kenneth N. Shrum, DDS	W. Douglas Vaughan
The Stitchery	

The following activities require a computer and Internet connectivity.

1. Visit a search engine on the Web to research the topic of alphabetic filing. Find two to three useful resources or facts related to alphabetic filing. Write a report on your findings and discuss it in class.

2. Visit the Web page for your city or state government. Can you find any information describing how records are stored (archived)? Record four to five facts about the storage procedures followed and share the information with your class.

3. Research online your telephone company's white pages alphabetic personal and business names listings. Find out what alphabetic filing rules are used to set up the telephone directory.

4. Visit a Web page for a foreign country. Research the alphabetic filing rules used to store records in the country you have selected. Write a report on your findings, and compare your results with those of other members of your class who have selected different countries.

Thinking It Through

Dig deeper to apply what you have learned.

1. Identify two or three key points you would make as a mentor to a new office assistant who prefers to file according to her own set of rules. One of your key points should be to explain the importance of setting and following a standard set of rules for alphabetic filing.

2. Research another set of filing guidelines other than those established by ARMA. Are there distinct differences between the two? Which set of guidelines makes more sense to you?

3. Look in your local phone book to observe the alphabetic arrangement of personal and business names. Can you identify the rules the publisher followed? Provide several examples of alphabetic arrangement that support at least three guidelines for personal names and three guidelines for business names.

4. What challenges might arise as you alphabetically file information organized by foreign names? Recommend several procedures to ensure proper filing and retrieval of files associated with names, titles, or subject matter in a foreign (non-English) language.

Subject and Geographic Filing Arrangements

7

Strategies for Ensuring Fast Access to Filed Information

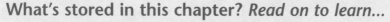

What's stored in this chapter? *Read on to learn...*

- When to use subject filing arrangements instead of alphabetic filing arrangements
- The steps for processing subject records
- The equipment and supplies used in manual storage systems
- Dictionary and encyclopedic methods of subject filing
- The advantages and disadvantages of subject filing arrangements
- The differences between master and relative indexes in subject filing
- How to use geographic filing arrangements
- The advantages and disadvantages of geographic filing arrangements

Just as there are many reasons why a record may need to be retained, there are a number of possible organizational methods by which that record can be stored to permit easy retrieval at a future date. Subject and geographic filing offer alternate means of alphabetically storing important records. As you will learn in this chapter, in many instances these filing systems are preferred to storage based on a business or individual's name.

Subject Filing

Questions?

What qualifies a record for subject filing?

When a topic or subject contained in a record is more important than the business or individual's name associated with it, the record may be stored alphabetically by topic. This is called **subject filing**. Subject filing is considered an **indirect access** storage system because it requires the creation and use of an index for proper storage and retrieval of records. Subject filing is commonly used for correspondence, reports, research information, inventory data, and newspaper or magazine articles.

Though you may not be aware of it, you are familiar with subject filing. The Yellow Pages portion of your telephone directory is a good example of information categorized by subject. If your friend referred you to her orthopedic surgeon, but all you remember is that his name begins with a W, how would you find the number? Can you imagine poring over the White Pages telephone directory to find the doctor's name under the letter W? It could take hours, or prove to be an impossible task. By using the Yellow Pages, you can go directly to *Physicians* and look under *Surgery* and then *Orthopedic* to find all doctors whose last name begins with W. Thanks to subject filing, your list of names is much narrower, improving the likelihood of finding the information you need.

Steps for Processing Records for Subject Filing

The steps for processing records in preparation for subject filing are similar to those used in alphabetic filing by name. They include inspecting, indexing, cross-referencing, coding, sorting, and storing.

Step one: Inspect the record. You must always check the document for a release mark showing that the reader is finished using the document. If the document does not have a release mark, ask the reader if the document is ready to store. Do not continue the storage process until approval has been given.

Step two: Index the record. Indexing is the most important step because the proper subject title must be identified. The subject title must be recognizable to all personnel using the system. Choose a subject title that covers the main topic of the document.

How to Determine a Subject Title

1. Read the document thoroughly.
2. Scan any enclosures.
3. Underline key words or phrases.
4. Decide the main topic.
5. Consult the alphabetic or master index to see if the subject title can be found there.
6. Check the relative index for possible subject titles, if the title is not found in the master index.
7. Code in pencil the subject title of the document for storage.
8. Check the general folder for other documents with the same subject if a matching subject is not found in the relative index.
9. Consult the originator of the correspondence if you are unsure of the subject title.
10. Make a new subject folder for records stored in the general folder if you find six records on the topic.
11. Add this subject title to both the alphabetic or master and relative indexes.

Step three: Indicate cross-references. If the document could have more than one subject title, make cross-references on the master index and/or the relative index to indicate other folders where the information may be found. The method of listing the cross-referenced subject in both the master and relative indexes makes coding a record easier and saves time.

Never use ink on the front of a document.

Step four: Code the document. Write or underline the subject title in pencil on the document. This will make the next step of sorting easier because you are able to see where to store the document. Remember: Never use ink on the front of a document.

Processing Records for Filing
- Inspect
- Index
- Cross-reference
- Code
- Sort
- Store

Step five: Sort all documents. Sort the documents in alphabetic order after you have coded them. This step saves storage time when you go to place the records in the filing cabinets.

Step six: Store the document. Storing is the physical activity of placing the records into the proper file folder. This is the last step in the processing of records.

Equipment and Supplies

Subject filing arrangements use the same equipment as alphabetic filing arrangement. They typically rely on supplies that include guides, folders, labels, and out indicators.

Equipment. Vertical and lateral filing cabinets are designed to house subject filing arrangements. Open-shelf storage is not recommended for subject filing arrangements because it would be difficult to locate folders in this type of system.

Guides. Subject filing arrangements require a standard set of alphabetic guides without subdivisions. Guides are made from pressboard or filler with tabs for labeling the indexing unit. The tabs are located on the top of the guide. You may wish to create a **special guide** for those subjects that are frequently used. Each special guide acts as a traffic sign to point to the location you are seeking.

Que**stions?**

Is open-shelf storage suitable for subject filing?

When six or more documents on a single topic accumulate in the general folder, it is time to make an individual subject folder.

Folders. Folders of heavy paper or plastic are available in a variety of colors for color-coding the records system. The tab extension may be reinforced because this area of the folder receives the greatest use. A general correspondence

folder should be made for each letter of the alphabet, which is placed as the last folder behind each alphabetical guide. All correspondence that does not have a subject folder can be filed alphabetically in the general folder.

Supplies for Filing
- Guides
- Folders
- Labels
- Out indicators

Labels. Labels, whether large or small, white or colored, identify the folder contents. Type folder labels uniformly, by beginning in the same location on all labels and using all caps or upper and lower case consistently. Never hand-write a label.

Out indicators. Out indicators are used for the checkout of records from the filing system, as a control procedure to keep unauthorized personnel out of the system.

Indexes

Subject filing requires the use of an alphabetic index. Before you can properly code a subject record, you must first look up the name of the record in the index. Never try to guess the name of a record. You run the risk of guessing the wrong name.

Two types of indexes are associated with subject filing arrangements: the master index and the relative index. The size of the subject storage system and the number of people accessing the system will determine whether a relative index is necessary.

Alphabetic or master index. An alphabetic index must be used with subject filing. The **alphabetic index** is sometimes called a **master index** because it lists all main topics alphabetically (see Figure 7-1). Each subject in the filing system will have its own 3 x 5" alphabetic card or be listed in a computer printout of the master index. Cross-references of a topic are included in the master index listing.

It is extremely important to keep an up-to-date master index. Every time a new subject folder is added to the filing system, the index must immediately be updated. This responsibility should be assigned to one records staff member.

Accounting Systems
Advertising Specialties
Annuities
Brochures
Business & Trade
   Organizations
Business Records Storage
CAD Systems
Data Processing Services
Display Booths

Figure 7-1 Alphabetic or Master Index for Subject Filing Arrangement

Relative index. The **relative index** (see Figure 7-2) lists the main topics alphabetically, with every possible related topic, word, and word combination shown on the main topic card or the computer printout.

The relative index shows all possible subjects that may be filed by a main subject topic.

SUBJECT	FILED UNDER
Associations	Business & Trade Organizations
Badges	Advertising Specialties
Bonds	Annuities
Catalog Designers	Brochures
Chambers of Commerce	Business and Trade Organizations
Commercial Artists	Brochures
Computer Graphics	CAD Systems
Computer System Designers	CAD Systems
Drafting Services	CAD Systems
Graphic Designers	Brochures
Insurance	Annuities
Mutual Funds	Annuities
Novelties	Advertising Specialties
Pension Plans	Annuities
Printers	Brochures
Profit Sharing	Annuities
Promotional Products	Advertising Specialties
Stocks	Annuities

Figure 7-2 Relative Index for Subject Filing Arrangement

Types of Subject Storage Arrangements

There are two arrangements for storing records by subject. With the **dictionary arrangement**, records are stored alphabetically from A to Z by subject. With the **encyclopedic arrangement**, records are group by a main topic with all related topics stored behind the main topic.

The dictionary arrangement (see Figure 7-3) is recommended for small filing systems of two or fewer filing drawers. There are no subdivisions in this arrangement. Every folder is stored directly by the subject name. Extensive training is not necessary for learning the dictionary arrangement.

Figure 7-3 File Drawer Organized in Dictionary Arrangement

On the other hand, the encyclopedic arrangement, which groups all related records under one main subject topic (see Figure 7-4), does require extensive training. The main subject is subdivided into more specific topics. Individual folders are stored behind the subdivision of the main subject. Indexes are extremely important in encyclopedic arrangements.

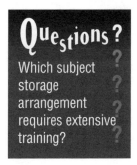

Questions?

Which subject storage arrangement requires extensive training?

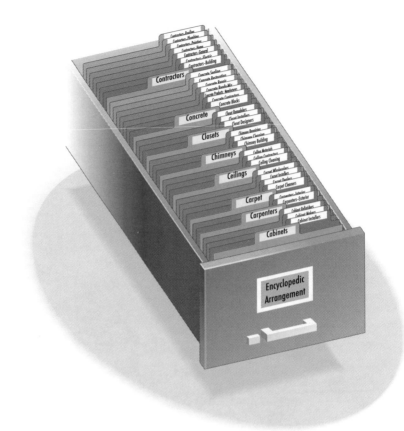

Figure 7-4 File Drawer Organized in Encyclopedic Arrangement

Advantages of Subject Filing: Ease and Expandability

Questions?

What arrangement lends itself to quick and easy retrieval?

An advantage of subject filing is that all records related to a specific topic are stored together for quick and easy retrieval. When researching a specific topic, it is especially easy to collect information from an encyclopedic subject filing arrangement. All the documents on the subject are gathered in one location.

This advantage is illustrated by the following scenario. Your superior requests that you find the records of all vendors who are the source of your computer equipment and supplies. If the desired records are filed in a dictionary arrangement, you would have to visually scan all the files stored in your filing system, or try to remember the names of all the companies in order to find what you need. Unless you have an excellent memory, this task would be difficult and time-consuming. If, however, the records you need are filed by encyclopedic arrangement, you simply need to locate the main subject, *computers*, in the filing drawer, and then locate the subtopics *equipment* and *supplies*. Following each subdivision guide, you will find the folders of all of the organization's vendors.

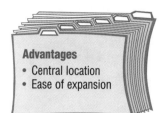

Advantages
- Central location
- Ease of expansion

Another advantage of subject filing is the ease of expanding the subject topic. New subdivisions are easily added in the encyclopedic arrangement and new folders can be made for new subjects and/or individual or business names.

Disadvantages of Subject Filing: Time and Money

There are several disadvantages to subject filing. Subject filing arrangements are the most difficult to learn, requiring individuals who use the filing system to be trained in proper storage and retrieval techniques. Even with training, it takes more time to store documents using this method, for the simple reason that each document must be thoroughly read to determine the subject prior to filing. Because no two people think alike, sometimes the "subject" is not immediately clear. Whoever uses the filing system must be familiar with the organization's unique way of determining subjects and the proper use of the corresponding alphabetic indexes.

An index is essential for subject filing by encyclopedic arrangement, to ensure fast, consistent storage and retrieval.

Another reason it takes more time to store and locate records filed by subject is because the master or relative index must be consulted for every record. Excessive cross-referencing of the alphabetic index can slow down the retrieval process.

Because a subject filing arrangement takes more time for training, storage, and retrieval, it costs the organization more to maintain. In addition, more guides are necessary, which adds to the supply expenses.

Disadvantages
- Difficult to learn
- Time
- Cost

Geographic Filing

With geographic filing arrangements, the fundamental unit of organization is the location of the customer. Geographic filing is frequently preferred by real estate agencies, international companies, mail-order houses, publishers, and companies with branches in many locations.

The relative index shows all possible subjects that may be filed by a main subject topic.

Que**stions?**

?
What is the
fundamental unit ?
of organization in ?
geographic filing? ?

Records stored in a geographic filing arrangement are placed alphabetically behind the main division (see Figure 7-5). The main division may be a city, county, state, region, or some other defined geographic entity. For example, an organization using geographic filing within the United States may choose states for the main divisions, with cities and counties as subdivisions. Alternately, the organization may choose regions, such as the East, West, Midwest, or Southwest, as the main divisions, with states as subdivisions.

Here is another example of how geographic filing might be used at an international company. The company maintains two separate filing systems, one for its international documents and one for U.S. documents, with a separate file cabinet designated for each system. The cabinet for international records contains divisions by country and subdivisions by city. The cabinet that houses the U.S. records contains main divisions for the 50 states, with subdivisions for cities. A general correspondence alphabetic folder is placed as the last folder behind each main division.

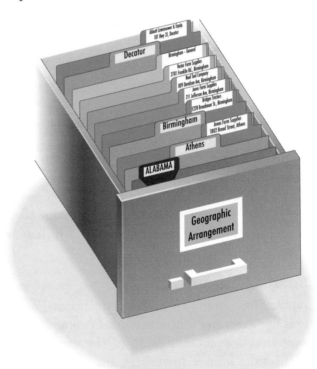

Figure 7-5 File Drawer Organized in Geographic Arrangement

Daily newspapers contain examples of geographic filing. The classified ads list homes for sale and apartments for rent within geographic regions. If the newspaper serves a large city, the regions are likely to be areas within the city (Northeast, for example) as well as surrounding suburbs. Organizing home listings by geographic location makes sense because people tend to know where they want to live, and they can skip past houses for sale in neighborhoods in which they are not interested.

Steps for Processing Records for Geographic Filing

The steps for processing records in preparation for geographic filing are the same as those used in subject filing: inspect the record; index the record; indicate cross-references; code the record; sort all records; and store the records.

How to Determine Geographic Location

1. Check the letterhead or the inside address for the location to file the document.
2. Scan the document thoroughly.
3. Underline key words or phrases.
4. Consult the alphabetic or master index to see if the location can be found there.
5. Code in pencil the title of the document for storage.
6. Check the general folder for other documents with the same location if the location is not found in the master index.
7. Make a new folder for records stored in the general folder if you find six records for the same location.
8. Add this title to the alphabetic index.

Equipment and Supplies

Geographic filing arrangements use the same equipment as alphabetic filing arrangements, including guides, folders, labels, and out indicators.

Equipment. Vertical and lateral filing cabinets are designed to house geographic filing arrangements. Open-shelf storage is not used with these filing arrangements because it would be very difficult to locate folders using this equipment.

Guides. Geographic filing arrangements require a standard set of alphabetic guides. Subdivision guides are needed for all locations. The subdivision guides require blank tabs for keying the titles.

Folders. A general correspondence folder should be made for each main division and subdivision. General correspondence folders are placed as the last file before the next division.

Labels. Labels to identify folder contents should be typed uniformly and not hand-written.

Out indicators. Out indicators are used for the checkout of records from the filing system. The same control procedures are practiced in geographic filing that are used in alphabetic or subject filing. It is important to keep unauthorized personnel out of the filing system.

Index

Geographic filing requires the use of an alphabetic index (see Figure 7-6). Each folder in this type of filing arrangement must have its own 3 x 5" alphabetic card or be listed in a computer printout of the index. The name, address, and telephone number of each individual or business is listed alphabetically with the proper filing title. Cross-references of a topic will be included in the master index listing.

Each time a new folder is added to the filing system, the index must immediately be updated. Without an up-to-date index, storing mistakes will occur.

TENNESSEE	CHATTANOOGA
	Chattanooga Records Management
ATHENS	Employment Resources
A-1 Office Equipment	Fast Print
Athens Office Temps	The Office Supply Center
Bob's Banners and Signs	State-line Printing and Supplies
Top Savings Office Supplies	
	DOVER
BRISTOL	Dover Freight Line
Al's Quick Print	Eagle Watch Printing
Bristol Stationers	Reelfoot Temporary Agency
Tri-Cities Motor Line	Reelfoot Lake Office Supplieres
Tri-Cities Office Supplies	
Tri-Cities Records Storage	

Figure 7-6 Alphabetic or Master Index for Geographic Filing Arrangement

Advantage of Geographic Filing: Easy Retrieval

As with subject filing, geographic filing arrangements permit easy retrieval of information because records pertaining to one area are grouped together. In the same way, storing additional files or rearranging the existing filing system is relatively easy because the information is clearly organized.

Disadvantage of Geographic Filing: Challenging to Learn

The main disadvantage of geographic filing is the difficulty of learning the system. The alphabetic index must be consulted whenever a record is coded. The system is vulnerable to misfiling when more than one location shares the same name, such as Nashville, Indiana, and Nashville, Tennessee, or Miami, Ohio, and Miami, Florida. Anticipating this type of mistake and helping records management personnel be aware of files with the potential for mistaken identity can help minimize this concern.

Records Management in the Real World

Sherry Lovett

Sherry Lovett worked as an administrative assistant in the properties management division of one of the largest insurance companies in the United States. The properties management division was in charge of maintaining the files for all of the company's locations throughout the country. Sherry was responsible for all the files for each branch of the insurance company, approximately 425 locations across the country. All of the branch files were set up in a geographic filing arrangement.

The country was divided into seven regions: South, Northeast, Midwest, Northwest, West, Southwest, and East. The states were then filed behind the region in which they were located (for example, South: Florida; Midwest: Missouri; Southwest: Texas; and so on). Individual cities were filed behind the states, with the branch office address typed on the folder label. Some of the larger cities contained more than one branch office. Cities with several locations included special guides, with each branch location filed alphabetically by street address.

Sherry appreciated the daily challenges of working with this filing system. She had to keep track of changing locations and to find the proper filing location for the numerous pieces of correspondence she handled.

Sherry now works for a large police department. She has advanced rapidly, and is now the administrative assistant to the chief of police. Her prior filing experience at the insurance company has helped her in learning the similar geographic filing arrangement used by this department. She has had to learn to identify all of the police precincts in the city, and to see to it that reports, correspondence, and all other documents are coded correctly and filed under their proper geographic location.

The police department is making good use of Sherry's expertise in geographic filing. She not only handles all of the chief's work, but she has the responsibility of teaching all employees how to use geographic filing.

For better understanding, review and reflect on the key points of this chapter.

The five steps for storing records in both subject and geographic filing arrangements are inspecting, indexing, cross-referencing, coding, sorting, and storing. Indexing is the most important step in storing records. Cross-referencing is a step used *only* when records can be stored by more than one subject. Cross-referencing is shown in the alphabetic or master index in both arrangements.

Vertical and lateral filing cabinets are used to store records in subject and geographic filing systems. The same supplies used in alphabetic filing systems are used in subject and geographic filing systems.

Both filing arrangements require an alphabetic or master index to locate the name of the subject. The relative index shows all possible subjects that may be filed by a main subject topic. Subject and geographic filing arrangements are more complex than alphabetic filing arrangements and require more extensive training.

An advantage of both filing arrangements is that all records on related topics may be grouped together for research purposes. In addition, both arrangements are easily expandable through the addition of new subdivisions.

The disadvantages of subject and geographic filing include training time and storage and retrieval time. The overall costs (time and money) of both filing systems make them more expensive than alphabetic filing systems.

There are two arrangements for storing records by subject. The dictionary arrangement stores records alphabetically from A to Z by subject. The encyclopedic arrangement groups records by main topic, with all related topics stored behind the main topic.

In geographic filing, the main division is a geographic entity such as a state or country. Subdivisions may include cities or counties; individual and business files are stored behind the subdivisions.

MEMORY FILE

True or False?
Rewrite each false item to make it a true statement.

1. Subject filing is used when the name of the subject is more important than the business or individual name.
2. Subject filing is a direct access storage system; no alphabetic index is necessary prior to storing and retrieving records.
3. The same steps used in processing alphabetic records—inspecting, indexing, coding, sorting, and storing—will be used in subject and geographic filing arrangements.
4. Open shelves are recommended for subject filing.
5. A standard set of alphabetic guides with special subject guides will be used in subject filing arrangements.
6. A general correspondence folder should be made for each letter of the alphabet in subject filing.
7. The master index lists all the main subject topics alphabetically.
8. A relative index lists the main topics alphabetically with every possible related topic, word, and word combination.
9. The encyclopedic arrangement of subject filing is easier is use than the dictionary arrangement of subject filing.
10. Subject filing is less expensive and easier to learn than alphabetic filing.
11. An advantage of subject filing is that all records in related topics are grouped together for research purposes.
12. Geographic filing arrangements store records by the location of the customers.
13. Examples of geographic filing arrangements are classified advertisements in the newspapers and multiple home listing guides.
14. Geographic filing requires the use of an alphabetic index.
15. Geographic filing arrangements are easy to learn and require little or no training for new employees.

Multiple Choice
Choose the best answer from those provided.

1. Subject and geographic filing arrangements require that an alphabetic index be consulted when indexing and coding the records and before storing or retrieving them; therefore, they are what type of access storage system?
a) immediate access; b) straight access; c) indirect access; d) direct access.
2. The two types of indexes used with subject filing are: a) main and secondary indexes; b) major and minor indexes; c) principal and relative indexes; d) master and relative indexes.

3. Another name for the alphabetic index used in subject filing is the:
    a) major index; b) master index; c) principal index; d) main index.

4. This subject index lists the main topic alphabetically with every possible related topic, word, and word combination: a) relative index; b) linking index; c) associated index; d) parallel index.

5. This subject arrangement of records stores records alphabetically from A to Z: a) encyclopedic arrangement; b) glossary arrangement; c) dictionary arrangement; d) vocabulary arrangement.

6. This subject arrangement of records groups all related records under one main topic, with subdivisions of more specific topics: a) encyclopedic arrangement; b) glossary arrangement; c) dictionary arrangement; d) vocabulary arrangement.

7. An example of the encyclopedic arrangement of subject filing is: a) a thesaurus; b) the yellow pages of a telephone directory; c) the business listings of a telephone directory; d) an automotive parts manual.

8. Which filing equipment is not recommended for subject and geographic filing arrangements? a) vertical filing cabinets; b) lateral filing cabinets; c) open shelves; d) none of the above.

9. A general correspondence folder for each main division would be used in: a) subject filing arrangements only; b) geographic filing arrangements only; c) both subject and geographic filing arrangements; d) none of the above.

10. Make an individual subject or geographic folder when how many documents on a topic are stored in the general folder? a) four; b) five; c) six; d) seven.

11. The five steps for processing subject and geographic records are: a) indexing, coding, cross-referencing, sorting, storing; b) indexing, coding, sorting, filing, storing; c) inspecting, indexing, coding, sorting, storing; d) inspecting, coding, cross-referencing, filing, storing.

12. The most important step in storing records is: a) indexing; b) cross-referencing; c) sorting; d) storing.

13. The step that is used only when records can be stored in more than one location in the filing system is called: a) inspecting; b) coding; c) sorting; d) cross-referencing.

14. A disadvantage of subject filing is that: a) it is the most difficult filing arrangement to learn; b) expanding the filing system is difficult; c) all information on a particular subject is located together; d) topics must be arranged in alphabetic order.

15. An advantage of geographic filing arrangements is that: a) no extra time is necessary for consulting an index before coding; b) they require little or no training of new employees; c) information is easy to research because all records pertaining to one area are grouped together; d) there is little chance of misfiling.

Terms to Know

Write definitions of these terms to increase your knowledge of the records management field.

alphabetic index
dictionary arrangement
encyclopedic arrangement
indirect access

master index
relative index
special guide

Make a Connection

Write or discuss your response to each question.

1. When would an organization choose to use subject filing instead of alphabetic filing?

2. What are the advantages of subject filing?

3 What disadvantages might you encounter with subject filing? Give a real-world example.

4. Why would you choose the encyclopedic arrangement of records versus the dictionary arrangement of records?

5. Explain the difference between an alphabetic or master index and a relative index. Why are both necessary for subject and geographic filing arrangements?

6. What kinds of organizations use geographic filing? Why?

7. What are the advantages and disadvantages of geographic filing?

8 Determine the guide name and folder of the following records.

Ex.ample:	Record	Guide Name	Folder
	Order for letterhead	Stationery	Letterhead

Make a Connection

Guides: Personnel Department
     Marketing Department
     Accounting Department

Folders:

Budgets	Applications – Buyer	Press Releases
Bids	Health Insurance	Ad Schedules
Petty Cash	Injury Reports	Public Relations
Vouchers	Employee Reviews	Promotional Material

1. parking garage receipt—July 19
2. resume of Linda Belew
3. Bob Jones's hospital bill—backhoe accident
4. Ellis-Grant Celebrity Walkathon sponsorship
5. listing of television air time for month of August
6. estimated six-month budget—Engineering Dept.
7. Timms Insurance Agency quote
8. bid for remodeling executive office suites
9. Ray Brock evaluation
10. Cravens Promotions catalog
11. Daily News article—Ellis-Grant Celebrity Walkathon
12. D & M Pen Company catalog
13. office supplies invoice
14. radio commercial schedule
15. reimbursement ticket—bakery

Make a Connection

16. Top of the Line computer bid
17. Apex Janitorial bill
18. Jesse Stewart application
19. Hurt on Duty claim—Andrea Pulley
20. K.C. Blair evaluation
21. 2002–2003 anticipated revenues
22. Advantage Health Insurance Co.
23. Jackson Elementary School Adoption
24. News Journal—C.W. Simpson article

The following activities require a computer and Internet connectivity.

1. Search the Web for an example of a business that presents information by subject with an encyclopedic arrangement of topics. Do you agree with the organization of the information? Try to find an example of a site that would benefit from reorganization, and make recommendations for more intuitive (easily understandable) categories of information.

2. Find a business online that presents information by geographic arrangement. What kind of business is it? Do you find the geographic arrangement useful, or does it merely slow down your search? Why do you think the company chose to organize its information this way? List all possible reasons.

3. Research online how the Yellow Pages of telephone directories are set up. What other types of directories are set up online using subject filing? Do they use a dictionary or an encyclopedic order arrangement?

Dig deeper to apply what you have learned.

1. In Chapter 5 you purchased the supplies and equipment for your records system at Jones Brothers Farm Distributors. As a distributor of farm equipment and supplies, the company sells products to farmers. Jones Brothers also orders equipment and supplies from manufacturers and vendors. You are responsible for the general company correspondence and personnel records of 40 employees. The general correspondence and the personnel records are kept in separate alphabetic filing arrangements. Mr. Jones has asked you to start a product information reference system. He has approximately 50 manufacturer and vendor brochures and catalogs stacked in his office. Explain why subject filing would be best suited for keeping a product information reference system. How would you set up the system?

2. As the manager of the Inner Peace Emporium, you are planning to convert all records from alphabetic filing to subject filing. This decision was made after a feasibility study showed that most records are requested by the type of stock, not by the vendor's names. Give the reasons it would be easier to locate records by subject filing instead of alphabetic filing.

3. As the records manager of the ABC Warehouse, you are planning to convert the records to a geographic filing system. ABC Warehouse has 45 locations in 8 states. Most records housed in the filing center are requested by their location. How would you convert the records from a straight alphabetic arrangement to a geographic arrangement? List the steps you would follow to reorganize the records.

Numeric Filing Arrangements

Ensuring the Security of Confidential Records

What's stored in this chapter?
Read on to learn...

- 📁 The types of numeric filing arrangements
- 📁 The steps for processing numeric filing arrangements
- 📁 The equipment and supplies used in numeric filing arrangements
- 📁 The purpose of an accession book and when to use it
- 📁 The advantages and disadvantages of numeric filing arrangements

The alphabet is not the only basis for filing systems in the business world. Arabic numerals (1, 2, 3, and so on) are also commonly used as the organizing element in filing systems. Numeric filing arrangements store records by numbers instead of name, subject, or location, and typically require a corresponding alphabetic index to aid in storage and retrieval. The use of numbers can add a layer of security to the information, making it difficult to locate personal or private records without access to the index.

Many organizations use some form of numeric filing system. For example, colleges often assign student identification numbers or use existing social security numbers to track student activities such as class registrations, scholarship money, grades, and so on. Banks, finance companies, savings and loans, and credit card companies assign customer account numbers that are used for following account activity.

State motor vehicle departments use driver's license numbers for storing the names of all legal drivers. They also keep track of automobile license numbers (which are actually alphanumeric, or a combination of letters from the alphabet and numbers) and of the person who owns an automobile. Law-enforcement officers anywhere in the country can access both numeric databases to learn the name, address, and criminal record of a driver, or to obtain information about a vehicle.

Types of Numeric Filing Arrangements

There are eight different types of numeric filing systems: consecutive, terminal-digit, middle-digit, chronological, decimal, alphanumeric, duplex numeric, and block numeric. Each system has unique characteristics that differentiate it from other numeric filing systems. Some of these systems will be familiar to you because you use them in your personal life, or you may have worked in an office that uses one or more of these numeric systems.

Consecutive numbering. **Consecutive numbering** filing systems arrange records in ascending order, beginning with the lowest number and proceeding to the highest number. Consecutive numbering systems are sometimes also called **serial numbering**, **sequential filing**, or **straight numeric filing**.

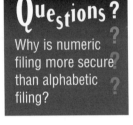

Questions?

Why is numeric filing more secure than alphabetic filing?

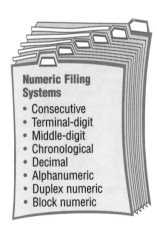

Numeric Filing Systems
- Consecutive
- Terminal-digit
- Middle-digit
- Chronological
- Decimal
- Alphanumeric
- Duplex numeric
- Block numeric

Preprinted or prenumbered consecutive filing systems are easy to use. Numbers preprinted on forms are the basis for filing in numeric order, beginning with the lowest number (placed at the back of the file) and progressing to the highest number (placed in the front of the file). The date of the record is not used as a basis for filing in this type of numeric filing system. Vouchers, purchase orders, checks, and invoices are few examples of prenumbered systems used by organizations.

File drawer guides for consecutive numeric filing systems are generally created in numeric segments of ten: 100,110,120,130. Each file folder houses a group of ten records; e.g., 100-109, 110-119, 120-129, 130-139, 140-149, 150-159, and so on (see Figure 8-1).

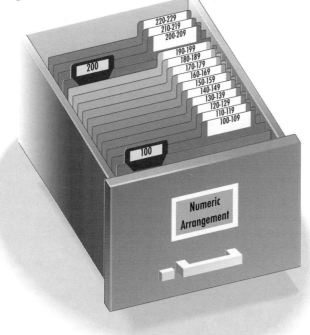

Figure 8-1 File Drawer Containing Numeric Segments of 10

Another variation on the consecutive filing system uses an **accession book** to assign each record an individual file number. All records are first indexed and coded alphabetically by individual, company, or subject name. The next step is to consult an alphabetic card index to determine the numeric file number. If the record is not found in the alphabetic index, the general alphabetic correspondence folder can be consulted next.

As with alphabetic filing systems, a consecutive numeric filing system contains a miscellaneous records or correspondence folder for documents that do not have a numeric folder. When six pieces of correspondence accumulate on the same subject, company, or individual, the items should be placed in their own folder labeled according to the next available number in the accession book. The name of the person, company, or subject must be entered in the alphabetic index along with the number of the new folder.

A consecutive numeric filing system featuring an accession book is ideal for conversion of an alphabetic or dictionary arrangement subject filing system. To make the conversion, you would begin with the first file folder behind the letter "A" and assign it the first number in the accession book (001). Information in the alphabetic card index would be transferred to correspond with the accession book and folders (see Figure 8-2).

Questions?

What filing system is ideal for conversion of an alphabetic arrangement to a numeric arrangement?

Steps for Storing Numeric Records

1. **Inspect** the record for a release mark before continuing the storing process.
2. Scan or **index** the document by scanning for the name or subject to determine how it is to be categorized.
3. Underline or note in pencil to **code** the document based on its name or subject matter.
4. **Sort** the documents in alphabetic order before consulting the alphabetic index.
5. Consult the alphabetic index for the number of the document file, then **code** the document with this number.
6. Perform a second **sort** to put the documents in numerical order before the final step of storing.
7. **Store** each document by physically placing it in the file folder.

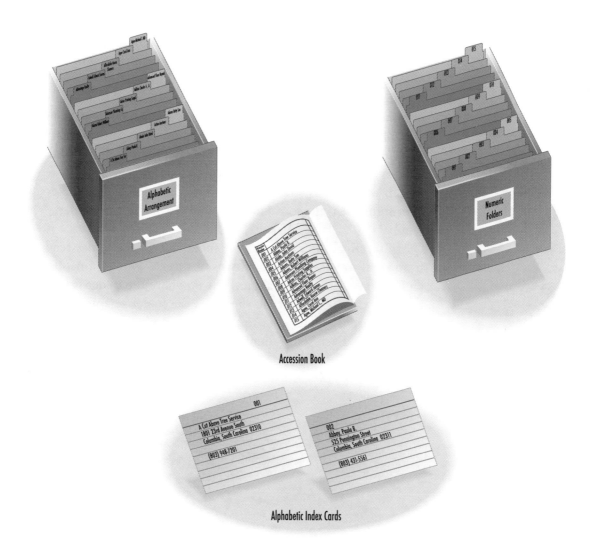

Accession Book

Alphabetic Index Cards

Figure 8-2 Elements of Conversion to Consecutive Numeric Filing System

Terminal- and middle-digit filing. Both **terminal-digit** and **middle-digit filing systems** are used when a minimum of 10,000 records needs to be stored. These systems are used primarily by large organizations such as hospitals and insurance companies. In terminal- and middle-digit filing, numbers are assigned by an accession book and logged into a card index.

The process of terminal- and middle-digit filing tends to produce fewer errors caused by misfiling or transposing of numbers when the files are established. Another attraction is that the filing system is easy to expand. Despite these advantages, terminal- and middle-digit filing systems are perceived as being difficult to learn, and their use does require time-consuming training. The system also requires special attention during the process of indexing and coding records for filing.

But what makes terminal-digit filing different from middle-digit filing? It is the location of the drawer, guide, and folder numbers as explained below.

In terminal-digit filing, the numbers on the file folder read from right to left in groups of twos or threes. The terminal (last) digits refer to the filing cabinet drawer where the folder is located; the secondary digits refer to the guide the folder is stored behind; and the tertiary digits refer to the folder number itself (see Figure 8-3). Each set of numbers begins with 00 and expands upward.

Que$s$tions?

What is the difference between terminal- and middle-digit filing?

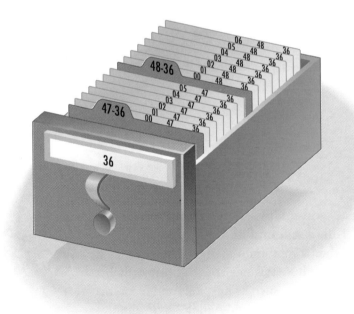

Figure 8-3 Terminal-Digit Drawer

Middle-digit filing is a modification of terminal-digit filing. The drawer number is the middle group of numbers; the first two or lefthand numbers are the secondary or guide numbers; and the folder number is located to the right of the middle group of numbers (see Figure 8-4).

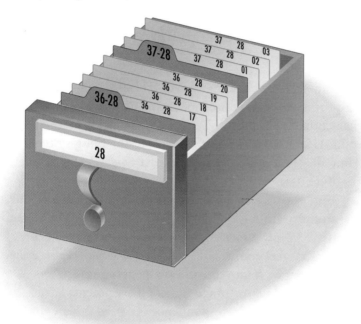

Figure 8-4 Middle-Digit Drawer

Chronological filing. Chronological filing refers to files organized around the sequence of time. There are three types of chronological filing systems: tickler or suspense files, pending files, and reading files. Chronological files serve as a memory device, grouping records in date order. Each chronological file has a unique purpose that may or may not be useful in all offices. Job duties will dictate which, if any, of these chronological files benefit your work.

A **tickler** or **suspense file** is a monthly reminder file of future "to do" assignments and appointments. For most situations, a manual tickler file consists of a file box containing 3 x 5" cards. The file contains guide cards for each month along with day guides from 1 to 31 and a guide card labeled for the next calendar

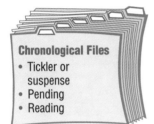

Chronological Files
- Tickler or suspense
- Pending
- Reading

year (for example, *2003*). Each record is placed behind the date the item will be needed in the future. To be effective, the tickler file should be checked just before the end of the working day or at the beginning of each working day.

Many computer word processing and office management software programs include a calendar feature that can serve as an electronic tickler file. To use this type of system, you must key the information into the calendar feature and check it daily as you would your file box.

A **pending file** is a temporary checklist for items currently being processed or requiring additional action. Upon completion of the action, the outstanding item is removed from the pending file and released to its proper location in the filing system. The pending file should be reviewed at least twice weekly to check the status of items it contains.

An example of an item in a pending file might be a Request for Travel Authorization for a trip to the ARMA Annual Convention in Montreal in July. Once the proper approvals have been obtained, all travel confirmations arranged, and tickets received, the request can be removed from the pending folder.

A **reading file** is a storage file of all documents keyed within a specific time period. Correspondence is stored in date order, with the most recent date at the front of the file. This is an in-house system and records are destroyed after a designated time period. The reading file is a timesaver, providing authors with easy access to keyed documents without interrupting work in progress or handy for use when the office assistant is not available (see Figure 8-5).

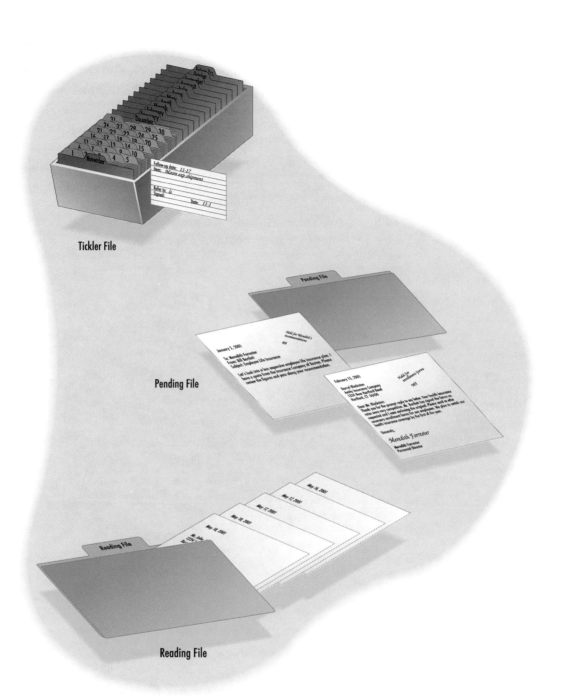

Tickler File

Pending File

Reading File

Figure 8-5 Files for Staying Current: Tickler, Pending, and Reading Files

Questions?

Who developed
the Dewey
Decimal System?

Decimal filing. The **decimal filing system** is based on the library classification system known as the Dewey Decimal System, developed in 1876 by Dr. Melvil Dewey. The decimal system can be divided into nine main divisions (100-900) with nine subdivisions. These subdivisions can further be broken into nine more subdivisions, with nine further subdivisions using decimals to distinguish them (see Figure 8-6). There is a tenth general division (000) for categories too general for the nine main divisions. The decimal filing system is used by the railroads, public utilities, governments, and libraries because it is an excellent storage system for large volumes of records.

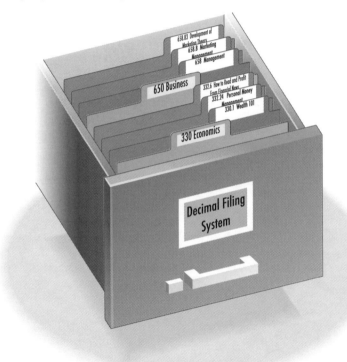

Figure 8-6 Folders in a Decimal Filing System

Alphanumeric filing. **Alphanumeric filing** uses combinations of letters and numbers as organizing elements. The main subject is assigned a whole number (100, 200, 300). All subdivisions are assigned numbers derived from the whole number (e.g., 110, 120, 130, and so on, within the 100 series; 210, 220, 230, and so on, within the 200 series). All records are filed alphabetically by subject behind the main and subdivision subjects (see Figure 8-7). Alphanumeric filing follows the subject filing encyclopedic arrangement.

An alphabetic index is used to list the subject and subdivisions with their number. A relative index shows the possible words and word combinations by which the records may be requested. The file folder label contains the subject name and number.

Alphanumeric filing arrangements are designed for easy expansion. The disadvantage is the extensive training required of individuals planning to use the system, as well as the extra time it takes to store and retrieve documents with this system.

Alphanumeric filing arrangements are designed for easy expansion.

Figure 8-7 Alphanumeric Filing System

Duplex numeric filing. Duplex numeric filing systems use numbers separated into two or more parts by a dash, period, space, or comma (see Figure 8-8). A combination of numbers and letters or all numbers can be used, with unlimited subdivisions of the main subject. Subject filing systems convert well to duplex numeric filing systems.

Subject filing systems convert well to duplex numeric filing systems.

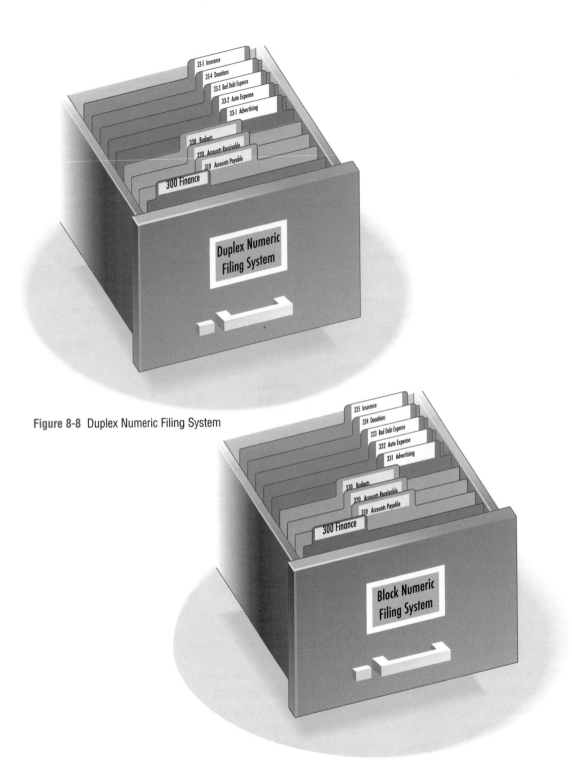

Figure 8-8 Duplex Numeric Filing System

Figure 8-9 Block Numeric Filing System

Block numeric filing. **Block numeric filing** systems are implemented when an organization wishes to create a filing system that encompasses yet differentiates among individual departments. Each department, such as Administration, Engineering, Finance, and Human Resources, is assigned a block of numbers for its division. The primary subjects are arranged alphabetically. Each subdivision is assigned a block of numbers from the primary subject number. The subdivision can be further broken into divisions and subnumbers (see Figure 8-9).

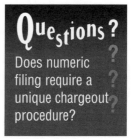

Questions?

Which filing system will differentiate among different departments?

📄 Advantages and Disadvantages of Numeric Filing

Advantages
1. Unlimited expansion.
2. Confidentiality—the label does not give information about a folder's contents.
3. Easy to locate misfiled folders.
4. Cross-references appear in the alphabetic card index.
5. Retention and disposal schedules are easy to create in consecutive numbering systems because the lowest numbers are disposed of first.
6. Numbers are easier to read than words.
7. Provides an efficient storage system for large volume of records.

Disadvantages
1. Expensive to set up.
2. As an indirect access filing system, requires reference to an alphabetic card index.
3. More time consuming to use and maintain than an alphabetic filing system.
4. Requires additional training.
5. Can result in problems if the accession book and alphabetic index are not properly maintained.

Chargeout Procedures

The same chargeout procedures used in alphabetic, subject, and geographic filing arrangements apply to numeric filing arrangements. When a folder is removed from the record center or filing cabinet, an out indicator should be completed and filed. Records personnel are responsible for maintaining the follow-up log that shows when and by whom a record was removed. It is a good practice to check the follow-up log daily. When records have

Questions?

Does numeric filing require a unique chargeout procedure?

Check the follow-up log daily to maintain control of records in your records center or filing system.

been out of the records center for ten working days, it is time to follow up with the borrower. This gives the borrower ample time to use the record and return it to its proper storage place.

Remember, confidential records should not be allowed to leave the records center without proper authorization from management. For security purposes, this type of record should always be returned to the records center before the end of the working day unless prior authorization has been obtained.

Equipment and Supplies

Numeric filing arrangements use a variation of standard equipment and supplies.

Equipment. Most numeric filing systems work well with standard vertical and lateral filing cabinets. However, vertical and lateral filing cabinets are not recommended for terminal-digit and middle-digit numeric filing systems because of the volume of records housed in these systems.

Open-shelf or mechanical shelf filing is recommended for systems with large volumes of records. Open shelves, however, are not secure and do not provide protection from fire or water damage. If safety and security are high priorities, mechanical shelves can be installed to house a numeric filing system. These types of shelves provide security and safety for a records system but are expensive to install.

Guides. A numeric filing system can make use of guides containing preprinted or blank tabs. Guides with blank tabs feature self-adhesive slots allowing the insertion of the tabs after keying. If the tab is blank, always key the information or use a stamp-numbering machine; never hand-write the information on the tab. Establish one guide for every ten folders in the file drawer.

A set of alphabetic guides (A to Z) and alphabetic folders is required for storing all correspondence not assigned to numeric folders. This set of guides and folders is stored in front of the numeric filing system.

Folders and labels. The folders and labels used in numeric filing systems are the same variety as those used in alphabetic, subject, and geographic filing systems. The types and colors of folders and labels will depend upon management's budget and preferences.

Accession book. The accession book is a log with preprinted numbers. When a new folder is made, the accession book is referenced to assign the next unused number in the book to the folder. The name of each new folder is logged into the accession book and the alphabetic index. When a numeric filing system uses an accession book, there is no alphabetic arrangement of folders.

The benefit of an accession book is that when a folder is missing from the file drawer, you can consult the accession book for its name. There is no guesswork to determine the name of the missing folder because you logged it into your accession book. It is also easy to notice missing folders when scanning the file drawer.

Alphabetic Index with Numeric Filing

An alphabetic index used with a numeric filing system lists all names, companies, and subjects, and the number assigned each file folder. Any cross-reference to other locations where records may be stored in the filing system is noted on the alphabetic index card. The alphabetic index should be consulted each time a record is indexed and coded for storage and retrieval. The alphabetic index must be kept up-to-date because it is the entrance key to the numeric filing arrangement. It should be kept in a secure location because it provides valuable and confidential information about the numeric filing system.

In most organizations, personnel records are filed by social security number or an assigned employee identification number in order to ensure privacy and confidentiality and make it more difficult for unauthorized personnel to locate information about a specific individual. The alphabetic index lists employees alphabetically, along with these numbers, in reverse or indexing order. The employee's address, business name or subject, telephone number, fax number, and e-mail address can be added if desired. Typically, the file number is provided in the right-hand corner two lines below or above the employee's name.

Questions?

Why should the alphabetic index be kept in a secure location?

To preserve efficient access to numeric files and the confidentiality of records, the alphabetic index should be kept up-to-date and in a secure location.

Records Management in the Real World

B & J Accounting

Betty Jarratt owns an accounting firm that specializes in payroll and income tax preparation. Betty handles the bookkeeping and payroll on a monthly basis for approximately 50 clients. During the months of January through April, Betty and her staff also do income tax preparation for outside clients.

Since B & J is an accounting firm, all clients' files are confidential and are filed numerically by state tax identification numbers. Betty keeps both an alphabetic card index and an electronic index with each client's name, address, telephone number, fax number, e-mail address, and tax identification number. Betty has two office locations, and she uses both types of indexes depending on the location where she or her staff are working.

Betty is required by the Internal Revenue Service to maintain copies of all income tax records she prepares each year. These records are saved on disks that are dated by year. However, some clients' records are on hard-copy files. Whether the record is a hard or soft copy, the record is filed by the social security number of the client rather than by the client's name. Again, this decision is dictated by concerns of confidentiality.

Betty deals with numbers as an accountant, but she also deals with numbers as an organizing factor when she is filing. Betty says she has always enjoyed numbers better than words.

Betty learned her filing skills not as an accountant but as a young office worker hired as an administrative assistant. While employed in a hospital corporation headquarters, she did both alphabetic and numeric filing for the accounting department. This experience proved useful to Betty when she established her own accounting firm.

For better understanding, review and reflect on the key points of this chapter.

Numeric filing arrangements store records by numbers instead of names, subjects, or locations. Numeric filing arrangements are confidential, and an alphabetic index must be consulted for retrieval and storage of records.

There are eight types of numeric filing systems. They are consecutive numbering, middle-digit, terminal-digit, chronological, decimal, alphanumeric, duplex numeric, and block numeric.

Consecutive numbering filing systems arrange records in ascending order, from the lowest number to the highest number. Consecutive numbering filing is sometimes called serial numbering, sequential filing, or straight numeric filing.

Chronological filing refers to files organized around the sequence of time. There are three types of chronological filing systems: tickler or suspense file, pending file, and reading file.

The steps for storing records in a numeric filing system are inspecting, indexing, coding, cross-referencing, sorting, and storing. Indexing is the most important step. Numeric filing requires a second coding and sorting.

The same chargeout procedures practiced in alphabetic, subject, and geographic filing systems should be followed in numeric filing systems.

An accession book or alphabetic index is required when establishing a numeric filing system. An accession book is a log of preprinted numbers used to assign records their file number. An alphabetic index lists the name or subject of the file along with the assigned file number.

MEMORY FILE

True or False?
Rewrite each false item to make it a true statement.

1. Numeric filing arrangements are not confidential filing arrangements.
2. Only a few organizations use some form of numeric filing.
3. Serial numbering filing is also called consecutive numbering filing.
4. Some consecutive filing systems use an accession book to assign records a filing number.
5. An alphabetic filing system is not necessary with any numeric filing arrangement.
6. Terminal-digit and middle-digit filing systems are used in small-volume filing systems.
7. An alphabetic card index must be used with most numeric filing arrangements.
8. There are three types of chronological filing systems.
9. A tickler file is a storage file of all documents keyed for a specific time period.
10. A tickler file can also be called a suspense file and can be kept both manually and electronically.
11. Decimal filing systems are used by railroads, public utilities, government agencies, and libraries.
12. Alphanumeric filing arrangements assign the main subject a whole number, with subdivisions having numbers within the whole numbers.
13. Vertical and lateral filing cabinets are not recommended for terminal-digit and middle-digit filing systems.
14. A second coding and sorting are necessary with most numeric filing arrangements.
15. Misfiled folders are easy to locate in numeric filing arrangements.

Multiple Choice
Choose the best answer from those provided.

1. Consecutive numbering filing systems are called: a) straight numeric, serial numbering, and continuous numbering; b) straight numeric, sequential filing, and serial numbering; c) straight numeric, sequential filing, and progressive ordering; d) none of the above.
2. This log assigns records a file number: a) number book; b) accession book; c) entrance book; d) none of the above.
3. Alphabetic and subject filing systems convert well to this numeric filing arrangement: a) consecutive numbering filing; b) decimal filing; c) middle-digit filing; d) alphanumeric filing.

4. Middle-digit and terminal-digit filing arrangements are used when this minimum number of records exists in a filing system: a) 20,000; b) 15,000; c) 5,000; d) 10,000.

5. A type of chronological filing arrangement is a: a) tickler file; b) reading file; c) suspense file; d) all of the above.

6. Which of the following chronological filing systems can be either a manual and/or electronic system? a) tickler file; b) reading file; c) pending file; d) none of the above.

7. Which chronological filing system is a temporary checklist for items currently being processed or requiring additional action? a) tickler file; b) suspense file; c) pending file; d) reading file.

8. The chronological filing system that is a storage file of all keyed documents for a specified time period is a: a) ticker file; b) suspense file; c) pending file; d) reading file.

9. This numeric filing system uses both an alphabetic and a relative card index: a) decimal filing; b) terminal digit filing; c) block numeric filing; d) alphanumeric filing.

10. This filing system is based on the library classification system: a) decimal filing system; b) block numeric filing system; c) alphanumeric filing system; d) duplex numeric filing system.

11. This filing system uses numbers separated into two or more parts by a dash, period, space, or comma: a) decimal filing; b) alphanumeric filing; c) block numeric filing; d) duplex numeric filing.

12. In this filing system, each department in an organization is assigned a block of numbers for its division, with the departments arranged alphabetically: a) block numeric filing; b) alphanumeric filing; c) decimal filing; d) duplex numeric filing.

13. Vertical and lateral filing cabinets are not recommended for which two numeric filing arrangements? a) block numeric and duplex numeric; b) middle-digit and terminal-digit; c) decimal filing and alphanumeric filing; d) chronological filing and alphanumeric filing.

14. Which two steps are repeated in storing records? a) inspecting and indexing; b) indexing and coding; c) coding and sorting; d) sorting and indexing.

15. Which of the following statements is not an advantage of numeric filing? a) Misfiled folders are easy to locate; b) It is an expensive system to set up; c) Numeric filing has unlimited expansion; d) Numbers are easier to read than words.

Terms to Know

Write definitions of these terms to increase your knowledge of the records management field.

accession book
alphanumeric filing
block numeric filing
chronological filing
consecutive numbering
decimal filing
duplex numeric filing

middle-digit filing
pending file
preprinted numbering
 system
reading file
relative index
sequential filing system

serial numbering system
straight numeric filing
suspense file
terminal-digit filing
tickler file

Make a Connection

Write or discuss your response to each question.

1. Explain why an organization would choose numeric filing instead of alphabetic or subject filing.

2. Explain the procedures for using an accession book and an alphabetic index.

3. Compare the similarities of and differences between terminal-digit and middle-digit filing systems.

4. Discuss the three chronological filing systems. When would each system be used in an office?

5. How do the steps for storing records alphabetically differ from storing records numerically?

6. Compare the advantages and disadvantages of numeric filing. What is your opinion of numeric filing systems?

The following activities require a computer and Internet connectivity.

1. Research the Dewey Decimal System and the Library of Congress system on the Internet. Share with the class any interesting articles you find in your search.

2. Find one or more examples of numeric or alphanumeric filing on the Internet. *(Hint: Examples of case law, research articles, and medical studies are frequently organized in this manner.)*

3. Use the Internet to locate equipment and supplies for item 2 under "Thinking It Through."

4. Research the Soundex coding system for numeric filing on the Internet. Explain this alphanumeric coding system. Who would use this coding system? Does it seem that the difficulty of learning the system would be justified by increased efficiency? What is your personal opinion of this system?

Dig deeper to apply what you have learned.

1. Contact a legal office or human resources department of an organization. Find out if numeric filing is used for their records. Ask the legal office if their cases are filed by client name or assigned a numeric case number. Ask the human resources department how employee records are stored (by social security number, employee number, or employee name). Be prepared to discuss your findings with the class.

2. Visit an office supply store. Compare the cost of setting up an alphabetic filing system to the cost of setting up a numeric filing system. List the equipment, supplies, and prices necessary for each filing system using a spreadsheet program. Explain your selections.

3. Talk with a librarian in your community about the coding system used at this library. Why is this coding system used? (Most librarians prefer the Dewey Decimal System to the Library of Congress. Ask the librarian about the Library of Congress system.)

Micrographic Filing Systems

Using Micrographic Technology for Document Storage and Retrieval

9

What's stored in this chapter?
Read on to learn...

- Why micrographics are a valuable document storage alternative

- The types of micrographic records available

- The equipment required to create, view, and store micrographics

- The process for storing records using micrographic equipment

- How to merge micrographics with computer technology

- The legality of micrographics

A 300-bed community hospital is running out of room in its records center. Each patient admitted to the hospital generates a file that quickly grows in proportion to complexity of care and length of stay. For a variety of reasons, the hospital must retain all patient records. **Micrographics,** a solution that reduces paper records to miniaturized images on film, allows the hospital to forgo an expansion of the records center and continue to maintain a manageable archive of patient data.

The community hospital described above is just one of many organizations eager to find alternative solutions for the storage of large quantities of records. Physical records take up space, which is an expensive commodity, especially at commercial real estate prices. In addition, paper records are fragile and can fade or disintegrate over time or through exposure to chemicals, mold, fire, or water. Add to that the fact that finding information within a large volume of records is time consuming, even when the records are properly stored. All of these challenges can be addressed through micrographics.

What Is Micrographics?

Micrographics is a cost-effective method for storing vast quantities of information in a limited amount of space. Through micrographic technology, words and pictures on a paper document can be greatly reduced in size and stored on film. The tiny miniaturized image of the document is called a **microform**. To retrieve microform images, the size of the microform must be

magnified using special equipment. When paired with computer technology, micrographics permit fast access to stored information, creating an important competitive advantage for businesses.

Questions?

What is a useful alternative for organizations running out of record storage space?

Through micrographic technology, words and pictures on a paper document can be greatly reduced in size and stored on film.

The History of Micrographics

Micrographics began as early as the 1830s with the development in England of microphotography by John Benjamin Dancer, an optician and manufacturer of optical instruments. The first microform patent was issued in 1859 to Rene Dagron, a Frenchman. He used his microfilm for the aid of his country in the Franco-Prussian War (1870–1871), and later for filming records in an insurance company.

Until the late 1920s, few advancements were made in micrographics. George McCarthy, an enterprising New York banker, developed a camera in 1925 to photograph bank checks. Banks nationwide quickly became the main users of micrographics. Until this time, banks returned cancelled checks written by customers and retained no proof of the transaction. This put banks at a disadvantage, leaving them with no physical evidence when customers disputed checks. George McCarthy's microfilm camera, the Checkograph, solved this problem.

The U.S. government adopted the use of microfilm during World War II for mail delivery and expanded its use following the war. The government became the biggest fan of micrographics well into the 1960s.

With the development of the computer and increased paper output, many other types of businesses began looking at micrographics as a way to reduce the amount of space needed to store documents. Currently, the biggest users of micrographics around the world are hospitals, insurance companies, engineering companies, and state and local governments and banks.

Questions?

How early was micrographics developed?

Types of Microforms

Five primary types of microform are used today: microfilm, microfilm jacket, microfiche, ultrafiche, and aperture card. Each type has its advantages and disadvantages as a mechanism for records storage.

Microfilm. The oldest microform is **microfilm,** a continuous roll of either 16mm or 33mm film designed to store reduced images. One roll of microfilm can hold 2,500 pages of documents. Microfilm is stored on reels, cassettes, or in cartridge magazines (see Figure 9-1).

Questions?

What is the oldest type of microform?

Figure 9-1 Early Micrographic Tools: Reel, Cassette, and Cartridge

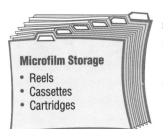

Microfilm Storage
- Reels
- Cassettes
- Cartridges

Microfilm is an excellent storage medium for long documents such as newspapers and other periodicals that do not need to be accessed frequently. The Library of Congress in Washington, D.C., microfilms very old books that have begun deteriorating. Most large newspapers microfilm their issues and sell these films to libraries and other organizations.

Microfilm records can be updated by splicing new sections of film into the continuous roll. The film can also be cut into smaller segments to produce a unitized microform.

The biggest advantage of microfilm is its storage capacity relative to its small size. Large volumes of documents that occupied numerous filing cabinets can be reduced to a roll of microfilm that occupies no more than several inches of shelf space. Microfilm eliminates the need for large storage cabinets, files, and shelf or floor space. Not only is it inexpensive, microfilm is also protected from fire and water damage when stored in fireproof cabinets.

The most significant disadvantage of microfilm is that it does not lend itself to easy updating of information. When updating is necessary, alternative microforms such as microfilm jackets, microfiche, ultrafiche, and aperture cards are more flexible options.

Microfilm jacket. A **microfilm jacket** is composed of two sheets of acetate or plastic sealed at the top and bottom and divided into horizontal sections that hold strips of individual microfilm images cut from roll film (see Figure 9-2). The jackets are the size of a 4 x 6" index card and hold 60 to 70 pages of documents. Some jackets hold only 16mm or 35mm film; other jackets will accept both sizes of film. On top of each jacket is a strip of tape for labeling the contents of the microfilm.

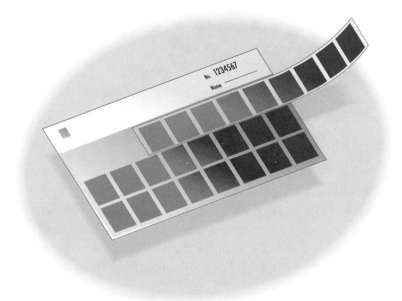

Figure 9-2 A Microfilm Jacket

Microfiche. The term *fiche* is the French word for index card. Thus, **microfiche** can be translated to mean a miniature index card, except that the card is actually a small sheet of film about the size of a 4 x 6" index card. The film usually contains 96 reduced images to a card. The images are arranged in rows

Questions?

How many images are contained on a microfiche?

lettered down the side of the card and columns numbered across the top of the card (see Figure 9-3). The rows and columns make it easy to locate specific images on the card, in the same way you would locate a specific street or town on a map.

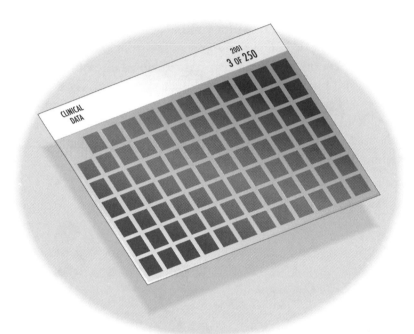

Figure 9-3 Microfiche

Microfiche has several advantages over microfilm. Cards have a tremendous storage capacity and take up less space than film. They can be filed as easily as index cards. They are a convenient and inexpensive way to send large volumes of information to another location.

Microfiche has streamlined records storage for many organizations, the U.S. government among them. Until recently, soldiers transferring to a new military assignment would be required by the government to carry their paper files to their new location, even if that meant hauling 20 years of paperwork. Fortunately, the military now employs microfiche to transfer military personnel records from one post assignment to another, giving soldiers a much lighter load as they begin their new assignments.

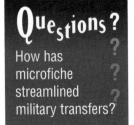

Questions?

How has microfiche streamlined military transfers?

Ultrafiche. Ultrafiche is the most extreme form of image reduction. A 4 x 6" ultrafiche card can contain 4,000 documents (see Figure 9-4). In one experiment at a religious publishing house in Nashville, Tennessee, the entire King James Bible was reduced to a two-inch ultrafiche square. The reduction process is so exact and delicate that it must be performed in a laboratory. It is also a very expensive process. Nevertheless, ultrafiche is a form of information storage that is practical for storing large publications such as catalogs, indexes, dictionaries, and encyclopedias.

Questions?
What kinds of publications are suitable for ultrafiche storage?

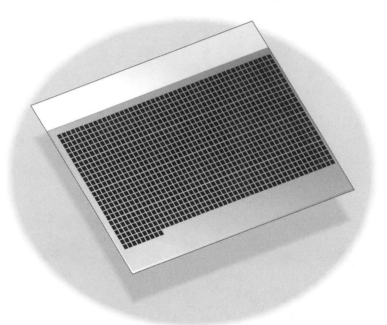

Figure 9-4 Ultrafiche

Aperture card. An **aperture card** is a rectangular cut-out card that holds one or more frames of microfilm. Information about the frame of film can be keyed at the top of the card (see Figure 9-5). The advantage of the aperture card is that it is a convenient storage and retrieval form for one-page documents and for engineering and architectural drawings.

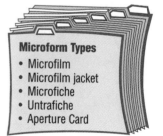

Microform Types
- Microfilm
- Microfilm jacket
- Microfiche
- Untrafiche
- Aperture Card

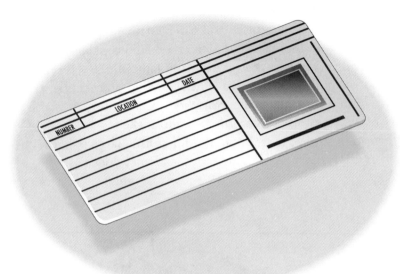

Figure 9-5 Aperture Card

Is Micrographics the Right Solution?

Organizations considering the addition of micrographics should answer the following questions:

1. What equipment is necessary?
2. Should the equipment be purchased or leased?
3. What records will be converted to micrographics?
4. How long will these records be kept?
5. Will production turnaround time increase?
6. Will filing system security be improved?
7. Will the micrographic images be legally admissible?
8. What personnel will be needed to operate the equipment and handle the records?
9. Will new staff need to be hired and trained?
10. Does the volume of records warrant the initial equipment, setup, and maintenance cost of micrographics?

Photographic Equipment

Various types of photographic equipment are required to create a micrographic records system, including the several kinds of cameras used in photographing records for micrographics. The camera chosen by an organization will depend on the types of documents in storage and the type of microform desired.

Rotary camera. The **rotary camera** has rotating belts that move the documents through the machine as it advances the film. This camera is used for filming checks, invoices, and sales slips, which require fast, efficient, and economical procedures. The rate of filming will depend on the skill of the camera operator.

Planetary camera. The **planetary camera** is a flatbed camera used for all types of documents, including engineering drawings. Documents are laid in the bed of the camera and the film is raised or lowered above the document to vary the reduction ratio, similar to the operation of an x-ray machine. The image produced by the planetary camera is superior to the image produced by the rotary camera.

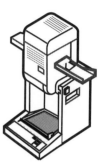

Step and repeat camera. The **step and repeat camera** is a flatbed camera used for microfiche, micropublishing books, catalogs, and parts and specifications lists. It is designed to expose images in rows and columns.

COM recorder. The computer output microfilm **(COM) recorder** is equipment that records electronic data from the computer and may be an online or offline component of the computer.

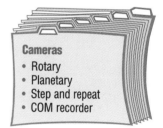

Cameras
- Rotary
- Planetary
- Step and repeat
- COM recorder

Retrieval and Viewing Equipment

Retrieval of information stored on microfilm, microfilm jackets, microfiche, ultrafiche, and aperture cards requires special equipment.

Reader-viewer equipment. This type of machine displays an enlarged image onto a screen for viewing. A **reader-viewer** may be a stationary machine, a portable reader that may be moved easily to different locations, a lap reader, or a handheld viewer.

Reader-printer equipment. The **reader-printer** performs the same functions as the reader-viewer, with the added capability of printing an enlarged hard copy of the document, usually 8½ x 11".

Enlarger-printer equipment. When oversize documents such as engineering or architectural drawings need to be viewed or printed, **enlarger-printer** equipment is required.

Retrieval and Viewing

- Reader-viewer
- Reader-printer
- Enlarger-printer

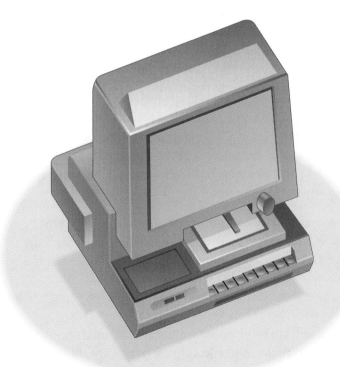

Figure 9-6 A Reader-Printer Machine for Microforms

Storage Equipment and Supplies

Microfilm is a good long-term storage solution, yet it is sensitive to certain elements and must be properly stored to ensure a long shelf life. Microfilm files must be stored in a controlled environment away from direct sunlight or sources of heat, as either can cause film to deteriorate. To ensure the protection of vital records stored on microfilm, many organizations choose to make two copies, one for active use and one for archival storage.

Questions?

Are there special precautions to ensure a long life for microfilm?

Roll film storage. Roll film is typically filed in multi-drawer cabinets or on shelves. Colored diagonal lines provide a simple method for arranging the rolls of film for chargeout and control purposes. Each drawer and roll container can be indexed and numbered, then placed in its location. A diagonal colored line is then placed on each row. A break in the line indicates where a roll has been removed. If a roll of film is incorrectly filed, the line will be broken and the misfile visible.

To ensure the protection of vital records stored on microfilm, many organizations choose to make two copies, one for active use and one for archival storage.

Microfiche, ultrafiche, and aperture card storage. Microfiche, ultrafiche and aperture cards can be filed in card cabinets, trays, or boxes using guides and out cards to control the records (see Figure 9-7). Heavy-stock alphabetical, numerical, and blank guides serve as dividers for the system and add support to the microforms.

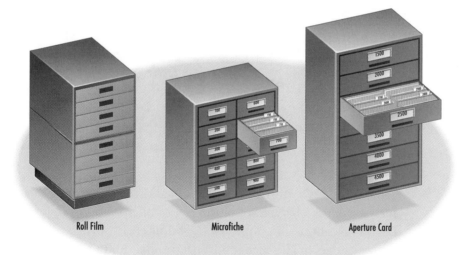

Figure 9-7 Storage Cabinets

Reducing a Document to Film

Several steps are required to create and use microforms. They include indexing and coding, processing or developing the film, and duplicating the film as needed. Each step of micrographics preparation is discussed below.

Indexing and Coding during Filming

During the filming process, microforms must be indexed and coded for automated retrieval. This is the most important step in the storage process of micrographics. Unless the record can be retrieved after it has been filmed and stored, it has no value to the organization. There are four methods of indexing microforms.

Flash cards or flash targets. Microfilm or microfiche can be organized into batches of information using **flash cards** or **flash targets.** The flash card acts as a title page identifying each batch of information or each subject of microfilm/microfiche.

Blip coding or image-count marking. This indexing method makes a **blip** or mark next to each image and assigns each image a number. A viewer counts the blips and stops at the desired frame of film.

Bar coding. This method introduces a pattern of clear and opaque bars between the images on film similar to the **bar codes** on food and clothing. A special terminal is necessary to advance the film and interpret the bar code. It stops the film at the desired location.

Odometer indexing. This method marks the distance of each image from the beginning of the roll of microfilm. An index at the beginning of the film indicates the **odometer** distance of the desired subject. The reader advances to the desired odometer location on the film.

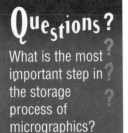

Que**stions?**

What is the most important step in the storage process of micrographics?

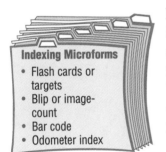

Indexing Microforms
- Flash cards or targets
- Blip or image-count
- Bar code
- Odometer index

Processing or Developing the Film

Once documents have been photographed, the film must be processed or developed. Film may be taken to a commercial service; however, most organizations purchase their own processing equipment if they plan to regularly convert records to micrographics. Today's processors do not require the use of a darkroom and are relatively easy to use. It is important that the film developer follow the manufacturer's exact recommendations regarding the temperature of the developing solution and the length of time the film is submerged in the solution.

The **resolution** of the microform refers to the degree of sharpness of the film, and will affect how well the film captures fine lines and details. Resolution becomes increasingly compromised as a document is enlarged. The more it is magnified, the more it becomes blurred or fuzzy.

Questions?
Can organizations process their own microfilm?

📑 Come to Terms with Microform Developing

Density: The amount of light that penetrates through the black areas. It is the measure of the contrast between the dark and light areas of the microform.

Magnification ratio: The measure of how many times the microform is enlarged to reach its original size.

Reduction ratio: Reverse of the magnification ratio; the measure of how many times a document is reduced from its original size to the microform size.

Duplicating the Film

Most organizations make a duplicate of the microform at the time the film is developed. One copy of the microform will be kept as a **master copy** of the original and stored for archival purposes. The second copy of the microform is called a **working copy** and is used for operational or daily purposes.

Contact printing is used most often to make duplicate copies of microforms. This type of printing is achieved by placing the emulsion side of the developed original film in contact with the

Contact Printing
- Master copy
- Working copy

emulsion side of the copy film, then directing a light beam through the original image to the copy. The copy film is then developed to produce a duplicate microform.

Merging Micrographics with Computer Technology

The integration of micrographics with computer technology produces the most efficient processing of information. Offices can save time and money by using computers to manage input, storage, and retrieval of micrographic records.

Computer input microfilm (CIM). CIM technology converts microfilm images to electronic signals on magnetic tape, which are then fed into the computer.

Computer output microfilm (COM). COM technology prints microforms, usually in microfiche format, from a computerized document file. The advantage of using this method over planetary camera to create microfiche is that COM units can produce many microfiche at an extremely fast rate—200 to 300 full-page documents in a minute. The COM recorder can accept data directly from the computer or from computer tapes or disks. The COM recorder thus becomes an alternative to paper printers as a way of producing computer output.

Que**stions?**

Is COM an alternative to paper printers?

Computer-assisted retrieval (CAR). CAR speeds retrieval of documents on microfilm through the use of the computer. Data stored in a microform contains an index number or code. Using CAR, when the code is entered into the computer terminal it is sent to a central filing system and converted into a signal read by the computer. The computer scans the filed microform until it finds the card with the matching code. That card is conveyed to an automatic microform reader and the image is transmitted back to the terminal to be viewed on the screen.

Computer Technology
- CIM
- COM
- CAR

Cost Effectiveness of Micrographics

Organizations can save from 95 to 98% of the space needed for storing paper records by putting their records on microforms. Additional savings can be achieved by reduced labor and mailing costs. Keep in mind that such savings are likely only when records must be maintained for five or more years.

Micrographics may not be cost effective for all organizations, especially small organizations. A feasibility study and cost analysis can help determine whether adding a micrographic system is a viable option versus maintaining a manual records system.

Questions?
Is micrographics cost effective for all organizations?

Advantages and Disadvantages of Micrographics

Advantages
1. Space saving—2 or 3 drawers of microforms equal 100 drawers of paper files.
2. Security—confidential.
3. Archival quality—lasts 100 years.
4. Combats technological obsolescence—little need to update.

Disadvantages
1. Difficult to update.
2. Start-up costs are high.
3. Extensive training required.

Legality of Micrographics

The Uniform Photographic Copies of Business and Public Records as Evidence Act of 1951 was enacted by the Federal government pertaining to the use of micrographic records as evidence in courts of law. This act allows microforms of business documents to be admissible as evidence in courts of law if the following conditions are met:

1. The filming of any files or records must be done in the normal course of business.
2. The records must be photographed in their entirety.
3. The microforms must be legible.
4. A certificate of authenticity must be included with the microforms.

Both state and federal laws should be checked prior to storing documents on microforms, since state statures can differ widely. Some laws require that the original paper document also be retained.

Records Management in the Real World

Marilyn Swing

The Metropolitan Government of Nashville has many records it must preserve for future generations. Marriage licenses, deeds, wills, court documents, and the actions taken by the government must be retained. For example, the County Clerk's Office has filed in the government's archives the original signed marriage application of President Andrew and Mrs. Rachel Jackson.

Marilyn Swing, the Metropolitan Clerk of Nashville, oversees numerous records in her department and is very involved in the records keeping of all city documents. Marilyn is active in the Nashville chapter of ARMA and knows the best preservation methods for vital documents. As the Metro Clerk, Marilyn has the responsibility for keeping all the City of Nashville's Council meeting minutes and distributing them electronically throughout the government. This includes archiving these records for future reference.

Marilyn feels that confidence in city government relies partly on records being accessible when needed, and that microfilming is the best storage method for the vast quantity of permanent records that must be kept. A few years ago, it was becoming impossible to continue to store the volume of paper documents generated yearly, so alternative methods had to be found. Optical disk technology has not proven itself as a long-term storage medium. Microfilming, a procedure that has been in use for well over 100 years, seemed to ensure the permanent storage capability that was required.

As optical disk technology experts continue to praise the newest technology and the "paperless" office, Marilyn Swing and other record management experts will continue to remind us of the foolproof, safer storage methods that use paper and micrographics.

For better understanding, review and reflect on the key points of this chapter.

Micrographics help to dramatically reduce the storage space required for paper documents. Through micrographic technology, words and pictures on a paper document can be greatly reduced in size and stored on film. The tiny miniaturized image of the document is called a microform.

There are five types of microforms. They are microfilm, microfilm jackets, microfiche, ultrafiche, and aperture cards.

There are four types of cameras used to photograph documents for micrographics. They are rotary cameras, planetary cameras, step and repeat cameras, and COM recorders.

Several types of equipment permit the viewing and printing of microforms. A reader-viewer enlarges the microform and displays it on a screen. A reader-printer enlarges and displays the microform, and also prints out a hard copy of the image.

Indexing is the most important step in the storage process of micrographics. There are four methods of indexing: flash cards or flash targets, blip coding, bar coding, and odometer indexing.

Micrographics has been integrated with computer technology for the most efficient processing of information. CIM converts microfilm images to a form that can be input into the computer. COM converts computer data to a microform output. CAR accesses documents on microfilm through the use of the computer.

Micrographic records can be submitted as evidence in courts of law, provided certain conditions are met. The Uniform Photographic Copies of Business and Public Records as Evidence Act of 1951 was enacted by the federal government pertaining to the use of micrographic records as evidence in courts of law.

True or False?
Rewrite each false item to make it a true statement.

1. Micrographics reduces images of text and graphic information in documents and stores them as tiny images on film.

2. Micrographics is a development of the late 1900s.

3. Banks are the only users of micrographics today.

4. Microfilm is the most expensive form of microforms.

5. Microfilm is stored on reels, in cassettes, or in magazine cartridges.

6. Microfiche is a small sheet of film about the size of a 4 x 6" index card.

7. There are no advantages to using microfiche instead of microfilm.

8. The term *ultrafiche* means the best quality of microfiche.

9. Aperture cards are used for storing one or more frames of film, usually engineering or architectural drawings.

10. Selection of the camera used to photograph records for micrographics will depend on the types of documents and the type of microforms used.

11. The most important step in the storage process of micrographics is indexing the microform during the film processing.

12. With COM, computer data is converted into microfiche or microfilm instead of producing a paper or hard copy.

13. CAR is the acronym for computer-assisted retrieval.

14. All organizations, large and small, can benefit from the use of micrographics.

15. The Uniform Photographic Copies of Business and Public Records as Evidence Act of 1951 pertained to the use of micrographic records as evidence in courts of law.

Multiple Choice
Choose the best answer from those provided.

1. A miniaturized image of a document is called a: a) minishape; b) microshape; c) microform; d) miniform.

2. The oldest microform is the: a) microfilm; b) microfiche; c) ultrafiche; d) aperture card.

3. This industry was the largest user of microfilm until the government began using microfilm during World War II: a) insurance companies; b) banks; c) hospitals; d) newspapers.

4. The most inexpensive form of micrographics is: a) microfilm; b) microfiche; c) ultrafiche; d) aperture card.

5. This microform usually holds 96 images, arranged in rows lettered down the side of the card and columns numbered across the top of the card: a) microfilm; b) microfiche; c) ultrafiche; d) aperture card.

6. The most extreme form of image reduction is a/an: a) microfilm; b) microfiche; c) ultrafiche; d) aperture card.

7. This type of microform has the advantage of being a convenient storage form for one-page documents and for engineering and architectural drawings: a) microfilm; b) microfiche; c) ultrafiche; d) aperture card.

8. This camera is used for filming checks, sales slips, and invoices, which require fast, efficient, and economical procedures: a) rotary camera; b) step and repeat camera; c) planetary camera; d) COM recorder.

9. The degree of sharpness of the film, the ability to record fine lines and details, is called: a) brightness; b) resilience; c) hue; d) resolution.

10. This refers to the amount of light that penetrates through the black areas of the film: a) density; b) thickness; c) solidity; d) compactness.

11. The process of making a duplicate copy of a microform is called: a) duplicating; b) contact printing; c) replicating; d) repeat printing.

12. CIM is the acronym for: a) computer input microfiche; b) computer inquiry to microfilm; c) computer inquiry to microfiche; d) computer input microfilm.

13. The acronym CAR stands for: a) computer-aided reversal; b) computer-aided reader; c) computer-assisted reader; d) computer-assisted retrieval.

14. Which statement does not describe an advantage of micrographics? a) combats technological obsolescence; b) lasts 100 years; c) little training of employees is required; d) two or three drawers of microforms equal 100 drawers of paper files.

15. Which statement is not a condition of the Uniform Photographic Copies of Business and Public Records as Evidence Act of 1951? a) filming of the records does not have be done as part of the normal course of business; b) the microforms must be legible; c) the records must be photographed in their entirety; d) a certificate of authenticity must be included with the microforms.

Terms to Know

Write definitions of these terms to increase your knowledge of the records management field.

aperture card
bar coding
blip coding
COM reader
computer-assisted retrieval
computer input microfilm
computer output microfilm
contact printing
enlarger-printer
flash card

flash target
master copy
microfiche
microfilm
microfilm jacket
microform
micrographics
odometer indexing
planetary camera
reader-printer

reader-viewer
resolution
rotary camera
step and repeat camera
ultrafiche
working copy

Make a Connection

Write or discuss your response to each question.

1. Compare the five types of microforms and give examples of the kinds of organizations for which each type would be suitable.

2. What would be the advantages of adding micrographics to an organization's records system?

3. When would it be totally impractical for an organization to consider the addition of micrographics? Provide a specific example of an organization that would not benefit from this technology.

4. Explain how computer technology can improve a micrographic system.

5. Why is it important to consider the legality of your records before filming them and destroying the originals?

The following activities require a computer and Internet connectivity.

1. Search the Internet to find information supporting the benefits of micrographics. Can you find any cost-saving studies or case studies that will help you learn more about the usefulness of this technology? Share your findings with the class.

2. Investigate a micrographics dealer online. Find out as much information about this vendor as possible: pricing, types of equipment, cost of supplies, suppliers, and so on. Retain this information for item 1 under "Thinking It Through." It will help you prepare questions for your visit to a micrographics dealer. After you prepare your questions, share them with your class and ask for any suggestions they might have about information you should seek.

3. Visit your state government's records management center Web site. What type of information is available there about your state's micrographics operations? Conduct an e-mail interview with the supervisor of the center about the functions of the center itself and about his or her job duties.

Dig deeper to apply what you have learned.

1. Visit a micrographics dealer in your community. Obtain any promotional brochures or information about the equipment sold by the dealer. Ask the salesperson for a demonstration of the equipment (you might request a visit to the classroom). If you are unable to see a demonstration, report to the class about the equipment you saw.

2. Talk with someone in a local government office, hospital, bank, or insurance company. Find out how the office records are stored. Are they microfilmed? Do they store the records in-house or in a commercial storage facility? Do they archive their records? Summarize your findings.

3. Check with your state Records Management Division. Ask about the legality of microfilming records in your state. What laws have been passed that have bearing on the use of micrographics?

Computer-Based Records Systems

The Future Prospects of Records Management

What's stored in this chapter?
Read on to learn...

- 📁 The features of computer-based records management systems
- 📁 How to work with databases
- 📁 Alphabetic rules applied to database systems
- 📁 How to use e-mail in conjunction with computer-based records storage
- 📁 How electronic records systems are defined and integrated with manual records systems
- 📁 Advantages and disadvantages of electronic records systems
- 📁 The legality of electronic records storage

Que**stions?**

Will the future of records management be paper-based or computer-based?

Computer technology has created increased efficiencies across nearly every category of business, including records management. The field of records management has been transformed by the introduction of computerized equipment and software that permit the transfer of paper records to electronic form. Many organizations are greatly reducing or eliminating their use of paper records, helping to further streamline and compartmentalize information management tasks. While paper records will not disappear from most offices and businesses any time soon, you can be certain that the future of records management will rely increasingly on evolving computer technology.

Computer-Based Records Systems

Computer-based records systems (CBRS) refers to all automated record systems that utilize databases for the electronic storage and retrieval of information. CBRS are designed to provide rapid access and retrieval of stored information to improve information integrity in paperless record systems. CBRS provide an efficient, convenient method of information management, virtually eliminating the need for paper records.

A **database** is a collection of information that can be organized in a variety of ways to meet an organization's needs. The main benefit of a database is that information that is keyed and stored once can be retrieved and manipulated many times for different purposes. Everyone given access to the database can use the information when and how she or he needs to.

Databases consist of one or more files of information. A **file** is a collection of related records. A **record** is a group of related fields containing information. A **field** is a group of characters combined to create one unit of data. For example, a human resources database may store all union employee information within a file. An individual employee's information is considered a record. A field might be the individual's salary or another pertinent piece of information (see Figure 10-1).

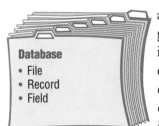

Database
- File
- Record
- Field

Emp #	Last Name	First Name	Middle Initial	Street Address	City	State	Zip
21043	Brown	Leland	C.	112 Kansas Ave	Missoula	MT	84311
19034	Guenther	Julia	A.	215 Bridge Wes	Lolo	MT	86308
27845	Oaklee	Thomas	E.	2310 Keating R	Missoula	MT	84325
08921	Avery	Michael	W.	23155 Neadham	Florence	MT	85901
30091	Latora	Gina	M.	13221 138th Str	Missoula	MT	84302

Figure 10-1 Fields Entered in Database Table

Databases do not automatically organize information; they must be designed to perform the functions necessary to meet the needs of the organization. A **database management system (DBMS)** is a software program that integrates data files into databases that control and manipulate information. The DBMS acts as a directory, showing where a document is stored in the memory of the computer. Information must be indexed and organized for retrieval, and stored either internally on a hard disk or externally on floppy or CD disks.

> Databases do not automatically organize information; they must be designed to perform the functions necessary to meet the needs of the organization.

Organization of Databases

Databases are created to provide fast access to information. Optimally, databases permit the addition, deletion, and reorganization of information by one user while simultaneously preserving the accuracy of the information for other database users. This is called **data maintenance.**

A DBMS is divided into two parts. The **file manager** controls the entry of the data and how it is organized in the database. The **report generator** searches and sorts the requested information from the database as needed by the users.

Databases utilize either sequential access or direct access retrieval. In **sequential access**, the computer must read all files until it reaches the requested file. In a **direct access** database, the computer goes directly to the location of the file requested; it does not read through other files first. This process is called **hashing**.

Questions?

What is the function of a DBMS?

DBMS
- File manager
- Report generator

Database Retrieval
- Sequential access
- Direct access

Questions?

?

What is data
maintenance?

?

?

Databases are organized in four ways: hierarchical, network, relational, and object-oriented.

Hierarchical database. Information in this type of database is structured based on a hierarchy, much like an organizational chart. In an organizational chart, the president or leader is at the top, followed by the managers, then the employees. All relationships in the organization flow according to the chain of command. Similarly, in the hierarchical database a main file or record is at the beginning and all other data files are built upon the main record. A hierarchical database is a sequential access database.

Network database. A network database is also organized hierarchically; however, it typically has more than one main file. This type of database can establish relationships among different files of data and allows greater flexibility for usage and access. The network database is also a sequential access database.

Questions?

?

What is the
advantage of a
relational
database?

?

?

?

Relational database. This type of database organizes data in **tables** or files called **relations** that can be further divided into **rows** or **tuples** and **fields** or **attributes** (see Figure 10-2). The advantage of relational databases is the ease with which new tables can be added to the database in comparison to hierarchical or network databases. A relational database requires complex software and a more powerful computer than these other databases.

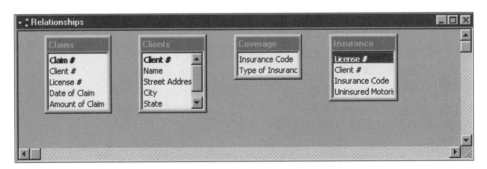

Figure 10-2 Tables in a Relational Database

Object-oriented database. A newer type of data storage program, the object-oriented database permits direct access to stored unstructured data such as video, audio clips, and photographs with data. For example, an object-oriented database containing student information could easily include a picture of the student within the personal information section.

Both hierarchical and network databases are slower than relational and object-oriented databases. To add a new field to either the hierarchical or network databases, the entire databases must be restructured because of the sequential access retrieval function.

Database Organization
- Hierarchical
- Network
- Relational
- Object-oriented

Database Management

There are three types of database management software programs available. These programs determine how the information contained within the database can be manipulated.

Database Management
- Software
- CBRM
- In-house

Database management software. These prepackaged programs, such as Access, dBaseV, R:Base, and Paradox, are available from various software manufacturers. To a certain extent, they can be adapted or customized to an organization's specific needs.

Commercial CBRM programs. Computer-based records management (CBRM) programs handle one or more functions of records management. Examples include the Inform and Frolic software programs.

In-house programs. An in-house program is custom designed and developed to meet an organization's needs. A computer analyst or programmer may write the program specifically for the sponsoring organization.

Selecting a Database Program

When selecting a database program, consider the following questions:
1. How difficult is the database program to learn?
2. Are the instructional and operational manuals easy to read and follow?
3. What data security features are possible?
4. Is training available?
5. How much does the program cost? Are there additional costs for program extensions?
6. What maintenance is required? How difficult is it to perform?
7. What ongoing support is available?

How the Database and Computer Communicate

A computer's **operating system** tells an applications program, such as a database, how to perform the functions of the program. MS-DOS was the dominant operating system from the early 1980s until 1995, when Microsoft released Windows 95. Windows programs, much like the user-friendly Macintosh operating systems, are designed for ease of use, with reliance on graphical, intuitive images to conduct tasks. Windows 98 and Windows 2000 have further refined functionality, and newer Windows versions are continually being developed.

Once information is stored in a database, it is listed in a separate file called an **index** or **directory**. This list contains the values of the fields and the disk address for each record in a file, usually based on the key field or several fields (for example, student's last name, first name, middle initial). Each group of records must be assigned a **file name** following the protocol of the computer's operating system. Windows file names can have up to 255 characters and spaces including the drive letter (usually "C" for hard drive, "A"  for floppy drive). The **key field** or **primary key** is a field in the database with a unique value that permits records to be distinguished from one another. Each file can have several indexes (alphabetical name, social security number, program of study, and so on).

Databases can be used to create forms, tables, reports, labels, and charts. You can feed data from a database into other office application programs without rekeying the information. Databases can save the user many hours of work by combining two or more applications into a single document.

An important function of a database is the ability to perform a **query**. A query is essentially a question asked of the database in

Questions?

How many characters and spaces can be included in a Windows file name?

order to solve a problem through retrieval of database information. A query requires a sort of the data, whereby a primary key or key field of each record in the database is selected.

Questions?

What is a query?

> ### Points to Remember When Setting Up Fields
>
> - Use up to 64 characters—letters, numbers, spaces, and symbols—for field names.
> - Do not include periods, commas, exclamation points, brackets, or accent marks in field names.
> - Key each indexing unit as a separate field.
> - Spell out symbols.
> - Key Roman numerals (II, III, IV) as Arabic numbers (2, 3, 4).
> - Key a zero to precede numbers zero to nine when the field is a single-digit number (e.g., 00, 01, 02, 03).

Records Storage in Computer-Based Systems

Records retained by computer can be stored electronically on disks, on magnetic tape, or on paper generated by printing from electronic media.

Disk storage. There are three types of disks used in computer-based systems: hard disks, floppy disks, and CDs. The hard disk is stored internally and permanently mounted in the computer. It has a greater storage capacity and processing speed than floppy disks or CDs. Floppy disks are 3.5" external disks that provide secondary storage. Like CDs, they are very portable. CD-Rs and CD-RWs are used as external storage devices for archiving data or for very large files.

Disks and CDs should be kept in plastic containers or albums with plastic sleeves at workstations to prevent accidental damage and loss. Computer media, which potentially can contain sensitive or confidential information, should be kept locked when you are away from your workstation. Disks and CDs should be put away when not in use, as magnetic shocks, accidental spills, or damage can potentially destroy stored information.

Magnetic tape. Computer data is also stored on magnetic tape, housed in canisters or cassettes, on open shelves or racks. Each tape should be labeled to include a file description, the date the file was created, and the retention period. A color-coded system may be created for easy retrieval and storage purposes.

Computer printouts. Most printed computer output is on standard 8½ x 11" paper, which can be filed like any conventional document. Some computer systems, however, still output the classic computer printout—a continuous sheet of information on manifold paper. This non-standard size document makes filing in conventional equipment difficult. Oversized computer records are filed upright in hanging files or using clips attached to a

binding. Both methods hook the reports onto horizontal rods that are then suspended from shelves.

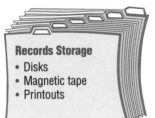

Records Storage
- Disks
- Magnetic tape
- Printouts

Data Security

Proper records management requires thought and effort toward the protection of data from loss or misuse. Because accidents will happen and information may be erased or lost, a backup disk, tape, or CD should be made of all valuable information. The backups should be stored in a fireproof cabinet or safe or at a separate location. The duplicate can save the organization the time required to rekey the information, assuming that it is still available. Codes or passwords assigned to authorized personnel prevent unauthorized access to important information.

The storage environment is a major consideration for all magnetic media. While magnetic data will not deteriorate, the physical properties of disks and tapes are susceptible to damage. Even static electricity from carpeting can cause electrical shocks and erase information. Disks and tapes should be stored in dustproof containers and protected from extreme changes in humidity and temperature.

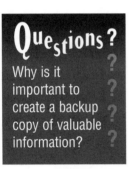

Que$_{st}$io^{n}s?

Why is it important to create a backup copy of valuable information?

Advantages and Disadvantages of a Database

Advantages
1. Information is centralized and can be queried to produce reports.
2. Data can be reused, requiring little or no duplication.
3. Data is accurate and secure.
4. Information can be accessed and retrieved quickly.
5. There is reduced potential for misfiling.

Disadvantages
1. Equipment is expensive.
2. The cost of database development is high.
3. Administration and maintenance are costly and time consuming.

Using E-Mail

The Internet, the "information superhighway," is a worldwide collection of computer networks allowing people easy access to unlimited information. One of the most popular uses of the Internet is **electronic mail** or **e-mail**.

E-mail is a means of automatically and electronically sending messages between computer users connected by a network. The sender can create a message, attach documents, spreadsheets, pictures, sound clips, and/or graphics, and send the message to one or many receivers' mailboxes. The receiver(s) can read, reply, forward, print, save, or delete the information. The message is stored in the receivers' mailbox until it is retrieved, viewed, and either saved or deleted (see Figure 10-3).

Questions?

What is e-mail?

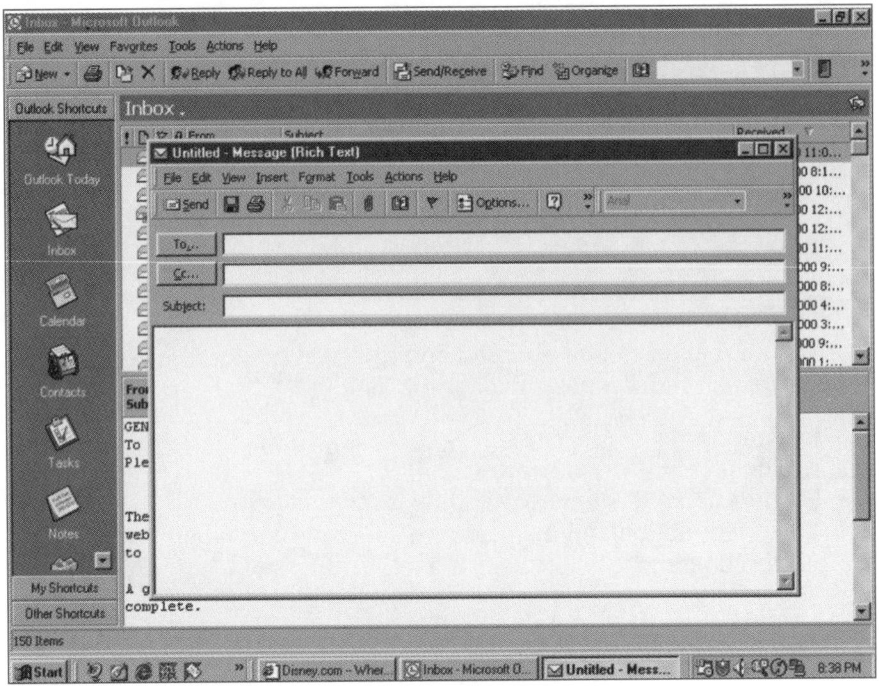

Figure 10-3 Outlook E-Mail Client

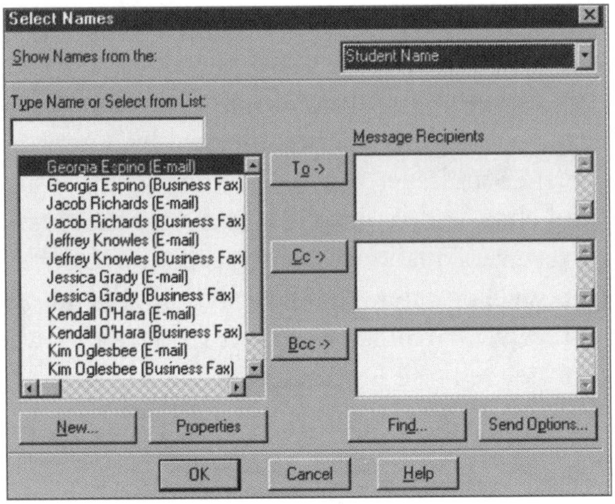

Figure 10-4 Select Names Dialog Box

Using the address book feature. The toolbar in the menu of your e-mail program has an address book. When sending an e-mail, you can go directly to the toolbar, log on to the address book, and select the name of the recipient from the Select Names dialog box (see Figure 10-4). His or her e-mail address will be automatically inserted in the *To, Cc,* or *Bc* box you selected. The address book can be used to store telephone numbers, nicknames, street addresses, and other personal information. Setting up the address book of your e-mail program and maintaining it may take time initially, but it saves many hours once the chore is done.

 E-Mail Writing Protocol

1. Always complete the subject line in the header, providing a brief description of the message context (see Figure 10-5).
2. Write in complete sentences.
3. Avoid slang and sarcasm.
4. Use proper grammar, punctuation, and capitalization.
5. Follow up with spell-check, if it is included in your e-mail program.
6. Proofread the message.
7. Always end your e-mail message with a signature line.

Figure 10-5 An E-Mail Message

Maintaining your e-mail files. Maintaining too many files on your e-mail program can slow down your computer and lead to sluggish performance. Clear your e-mail Inbox file of unnecessary items on a daily or weekly basis by deleting or trashing them. The Sent Item file should also be checked and sent messages deleted regularly. Print and store a paper copy of important e-mails as needed. Using folders, organize and file e-mails you wish to save.

E-mail, when used properly, provides a low-cost, fast, convenient method of exchanging information. Junk mail can become a problem, as can the temptation to spend time corresponding with friends. E-mail is a business tool to improve office efficiency and should be used according to your organization's guidelines.

Creating Storage Folders within your E-Mail Program

You can create special folders within some e-mail programs in which to save sent or received messages. Here is how to create folders if you are using Microsoft Outlook for your e-mail:

1. Click File on the menu bar, and then click New Folder on the drop-down menu.
2. Type the desired new folder name in the Create New Folder dialog box (see Figure 10-6).
3. Click OK when you are satisfied with the name you have provided.
4. Drag and drop the messages into the folder.

Figure 10-6 Create New Folder Dialog Box

Electronic Document Management Systems

Electronic document management systems (EDMS) create electronic images of paper records using **electronic imaging** or **optical disk technology.** EDMS increase productivity by combining technology with document processing.

Optical disks use a laser beam, rather than the magnetism employed by floppy disks, to store information. The laser beam burns data onto the surface of the optical disk.

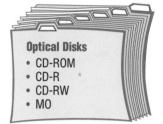

There are several types of optical disks. The **CD-ROM** is the most commonly used and least expensive optical disk. CD-ROM stands for Compact Disk-Read Only Memory. Information stored on a CD-ROM cannot be erased, nor can a CD-ROM be recorded on the user's computer. A **CD-R** (Compact Disk-Recordable) can be recorded by the user. Documents can be updated by adding a new version on the disk; older versions are ignored but not erased as new versions are added. A **CD-RW** (Compact Disk-ReWritable) can be recorded, erased, and reused by the user in a way similar to a floppy disk, but with greater storage capacity. The **MO (magneto-optical) disk** combines the magnetic features of tapes and disks with optical technology for greater storage capability.

Optical disks are permanent storage media for audio, video, digital, and digitized data. They are durable instruments that, unlike floppy disks, are not susceptible to humidity, dust, fingerprints, or magnets.

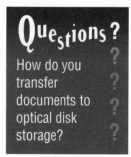

Optical Disks
- CD-ROM
- CD-R
- CD-RW
- MO

Equipment and Process for Optical Disk Storage

Special equipment is necessary to transfer documents, graphics, handwritten documents, and pictures to optical disk storage. The required equipment includes an optical character recognition (OCR) scanner, an optical disk drive or jukebox, and a personal or networked computer with imaging software.

Optical character recognition. OCR technology is a fast way to create electronic images of paper documents. When scanned with an OCR scanner, a document is converted into a digital image and stored on an optical disk. When scanning is complete, the

Questions?

How do you transfer documents to optical disk storage?

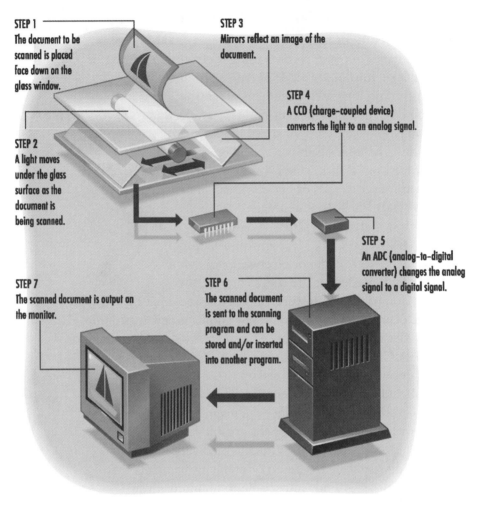

STEP 1
The document to be scanned is placed face down on the glass window.

STEP 2
A light moves under the glass surface as the document is being scanned.

STEP 3
Mirrors reflect an image of the document.

STEP 4
A CCD (charge-coupled device) converts the light to an analog signal.

STEP 5
An ADC (analog-to-digital converter) changes the analog signal to a digital signal.

STEP 6
The scanned document is sent to the scanning program and can be stored and/or inserted into another program.

STEP 7
The scanned document is output on the monitor.

Figure 10-7 How a Scanner Works

document can be reviewed prior to saving (see Figure 10-7). The file is then saved by file name in the index of the directory.

To retrieve a saved document, the index is consulted. The index will consist of content words of the scanned documents for easy search and retrieval. The image will appear on the screen as a full-page replica of the original document for viewing or printing. A printer may be a component of the system or accessible as a peripheral device of a network system.

Optical disks may be stored in a single- or double-drive unit if the system is not networked, permitting access to the imaging system by only one user at a time. Networked imaging systems feature an optical disk jukebox capable of holding 5 to 20 optical disks. The directory of each optical disk is stored in the computer and must be selected in order to retrieve a file contained within it.

Computer output to laser disk (COLD). COLD is a process of scanning paper documents to create electronic records saved on optical or magneto-optical disk. The benefit of COLD is that all employees networked throughout an organization at various locations can access the records quickly and easily.

Advantages and Disadvantages of Electronic Imaging

Advantages
1. Storage is accurate and reliable.
2. Processing time is quick.
3. Any form of document can be stored (text, graphics, microform, and so on).
4. Misfiling of documents is reduced.
5. Documents can be scanned rather than keyed for storage.

Disadvantages
1. System is expensive to purchase and install.
2. Electronic copies are not legal evidence in all situations.
3. Employee training is required.
4. Optical disk life span is just 10 years, compared to 100 years for microform.

Evaluation of Electronic Systems

Electronic records systems can save an organization money on labor cost, retrieval time, and mailing expense for records that must be retained for a long period of time. Installation of an electronic records system will not produce a rapid return on investment. Rather, the savings will be generated over a lengthy period through increased productivity of the organization's personnel.

A feasibility study can help to determine whether an electronic system is warranted. Unless a cost analysis demonstrates justification for expansion of the present records system to EDMS, the organization should stay with its present arrangement.

Is EDMS the Right Solution?

Organizations considering implementing an EDMS should answer the following questions:

1. Will the equipment pay for itself?
2. What equipment is necessary?
3. Should equipment be leased or purchased?
4. What records will be converted to optical disk?
5. What staff will be trained?
6. Will new staff be required?
7. Are there enough records to warrant the system?
8. What benefits will the organization achieve from the system?

Legality of Electronic Systems

The Uniform Photographic Copies of Business and Public Records as Evidence Act of 1951 was introduced in Chapter 9 with regard to filming records on microforms. This law also applies to records stored on optical disks. The law states that records stored on

optical disks must be scanned during the normal course of business and scanned in their entirety. The scanned document must be legible and a certificate of authenticity must be included with the scanned document. State and federal laws should be checked prior to storing documents on optical disk, to ensure their legality in the event of legal action.

Records Management in the Real World

R. Stephen Richards

R. Stephen (Steve) Richards is an information manager and owner of Richards & Richards Office Records Management, Inc., a commercial records storage company. Steve says, "I store records for a living. I look for the cheapest technology in which to store documents. There is still nothing as cost effective as paper. Paper is the most widely used storage medium, as 95% of all records are stored on paper, 4% on microfilm, and 1% are listed as other, and this includes optical disk, according to the Association of Records Managers and Administrators (ARMA)."

Micrographics is the most stable electronic storage medium because it has remained virtually the same for the past 50 years, with little change in equipment. A disadvantage of optical disk storage is that every 5 years the computer equipment and operating systems must be upgraded and the data stored on the disks migrated to new disks in order to keep up with technological changes.

Both micrographics and optical disk technology require hiring highly qualified personnel to do the scanning and indexing of the documents. This is a major but necessary cost for any organization. As Steve says, "If the documents are not properly indexed (inventoried), you will have nothing but wasted disks or film. This employee must know the company, the equipment, the types of documents, and the users of the documents, as well as how to inventory and place into logical order the documents he or she scans or films."

A May 18, 1998, *Business Week* article, "Microfilm: Here Today, Here Tomorrow," discusses not only optical disk technology as being hardware and software dependent, but also the decay or disintegration of optical disks. The author of this article believes that, besides paper, micrographics will remain the only long-term storage medium through which future generations will view important data.

Cost is always a major consideration for any organization. Steve pointed out how long it takes to get a return on the money invested by an organization using micrographics and optical disk storage in comparison to one cubic foot of paper documents stored. It will take 12 years before you will see a return of your money with micrographics and 27 years with optical disk storage. In addition, optical disk storage requires that you retain a backup replica of the document. What is the backup? Usually the original paper document.

Steve does believe that optical disk storage has a place in the office environment. It is a great medium for storing working records when you have a large volume that needs to be accessed easily and quickly in multiple locations, like the government records discussed in Chapter 9.

For better understanding, review and reflect on the key points of this chapter.

Computer-based records systems include all automated record systems. They are designed to provide rapid access to and retrieval of stored information without the need for paper documents. Information is stored in CBRS on media that include hard disks, floppy disks, and CD-ROMs.

A database is a collection of information stored in a computer system that permits the addition, deletion, and reorganization of stored information. Once information is keyed it can be accessed many times.

Databases are used to create reports, tables, forms, labels, and charts. Information can be linked from a database to other office application programs. Databases are able to query information through defined sorts.

E-mail is one of the most popular uses of the Internet. It is a quick and efficient means of sending messages electronically between computer users connected by a network. E-mail is a convenient, low-cost business tool used to improve office efficiency.

Electronic imaging creates storable electronic images of paper documents on optical disk through the use of optical character recognition (OCR) scanning equipment. Electronic document management systems (EDMS) increase productivity by combining computer technology with document processing. This technology is an expensive records system to initiate; a feasibility study should be conducted to justify installation.

The same laws apply to electronic imaging that apply to micrographics. State and federal laws should be checked prior to storing documents on optical disk, to ensure their legality in the event of legal action.

True or False?
Rewrite each false item to make it a true statement.

1. Computer-based records systems eliminate the need for paper records.

2. The main objective of CBRS is that once information is keyed it does not need to be rekeyed.

3. Databases are collections of information organized in a variety of ways to meet the needs of an organization.

4. A record is a group of characters combined to create one unit of data.

5. Sequential access permits you to go directly to the location of the file requested; it does not read through other files first.

6. The operating system of the computer tells an application program how to perform the functions of the program.

7. The *key field* is a field in the database with a unique value that permits records to be distinguished from each other.

8. A query is one of the most important functions of a database.

9. E-mail is a low-cost, fast, convenient method of sending information.

10. Using the internet and e-mail for personal employee use during business hours has not become a problem in the business world.

11. EDMS is also called optical disk technology or electronic imaging.

12. No special equipment is needed for electronic imaging.

13. Optical disks use light beams to store information, whereas floppy disks use magnetism.

14. The CD-ROM is the most commonly used and least expensive optical disk.

15. There are no laws governing the use of electronic imaging.

Multiple Choice
Choose the best answer from those provided.

1. The acronym CBRS refers to all: a) automated records; b) automatic records; c) authorized records; d) authentic records.

2. A collection of information organized in a variety of ways to meet an organization's needs is called a: a) file; b) database; c) report; d) document.

3 A collection of related records is called a/an: a) file; b) field; c) folder; d) index.

4. A group of related fields containing information is called a: a) field; b) file; c) folder; d) record.

5. DBMS consists of two parts: a) the file manager and the data maintenance manager; b) the file manager and the report generator; c) the file manager and the network generator; d) the report generator and the data maintenance manager.

6. In direct access, the process of going directly to the location of the requested file is called: a) sorting; b) reading; c) hashing; d) batching.

7. A separate file used to record the location of a record in storage media is called the directory or the: a) listing; b) catalog; c) file; d) index.

8. Another name for the key field is: a) prime key; b) initial key; c) first key; d) primary key.

9. Protecting data from being lost or misused is called: a) data protection, b) data security; c) data safety; d) data maintenance.

10. Which of the following is *not* a consideration when selecting a database program: a) ease of learning; b) cost of program and add-ons; c) name of vendor; d) availability of training.

11. Which of the following is *not* an advantage of a database: a) reduction of misfiling; b) faster access and retrieval; c) more paper documentation; d) less duplication of data.

12. Which of the following is incorrect e-mail protocol: a) complete the subject line; b) use slang and sarcasm; c) proofread the message; d) write in complete sentences.

13. The acronym EDMS means: a) electrical document management system; b) electronic device management system; c) electrical device management system; d) electronic document management system.

14. When conducting a feasibility study regarding electronic imaging, which of the following would *not* be a consideration: a) cost of equipment; b) volume of records to store; c) the benefits; d) the name of the employee you plan to hire.

15. Which of the following is *not* an advantage of electronic imaging: a) quicker processing time; b) reduction of misfiled documents; c) accurate and reliable storage; d) training time.

Terms to Know

Write definitions of these terms to increase your knowledge of the records management field.

attribute
automated record system
CD-R
CD-ROM
CD-RW
computer-based records management system
computer output to laser disk
data maintenance
data security
database
direct access
directory
erasable optical disk

electronic document management system
electronic imaging
electronic mail
e-mail
field
file
file manager
file name
floppy disk
hard disk
hashing
hierarchical database
index
magneto-optical disk
network database

object-oriented database
operating system
optical disk
primary key
query
record
relational database
relations
report generator
row
sequential access
subdirectory
table
tuple

Make a Connection

Write or discuss your response to each question.

1. What is CBRS?

2. Define a database.

3. Why is DBMS important to an organization?

4. Explain the four ways databases can be designed.

5. How is information organized in databases?

6. What is the importance of e-mail?

7. Make a list of rules to follow when using e-mail.

8. Explain electronic imaging.

9. How can electronic imaging benefit an organization?

10. Why would an organization decide against an EDMS?

The following activities require a computer and Internet connectivity.

1. Find an article on the Internet dealing with electronic records. Read and write a brief synopsis of the article to give as a report to the class.

2. Research packaged database software programs using the Internet. Select one program and evaluate its utility as a method for storing customer records on a small scale.

3. Set up an address book in e-mail. Write an informative e-mail to your friends following the protocol for e-mails found in this chapter. Print both the e-mail and your address book

4. Research federal and state regulations online for legislation pertaining to electronic document systems or optical disk storage. Did you find any laws regarding the use of optical disk storage? If so, write a summary of their content, and share the information with your class.

5. 5. Investigate an electronic imaging vendor, just as you did in Chapter 9 for micrographics equipment. Your findings will provide the background information for your vendor visit in item 2 under "Thinking It Through."

Dig deeper to apply what you have learned.

1. If you were to create a database of information around the individuals in your class, what fields of information would you include? Suggest one or two queries that your instructor might use to generate a report.

2. Visit an electronic imaging vendor and obtain information about the equipment and cost necessary to set up an EDMS. If possible, ask to see a demonstration of the equipment. Write a summary of your visit.

3. Create an address book of your personal records using a database. The database should include name, address, telephone number, e-mail address, birthday, and other important information. Print a hard copy of your project.

Glossary

accession book A log with preprinted numbers used to assign the next unused number to a folder in numeric filing arrangements.

active record A record that is frequently used in filing systems to perform the operations of an organization.

alphabetic card system Index card record for storing frequently used information such as names, addresses, and telephone numbers of customers, clients, suppliers, and vendors, as well as for locating the subject, geographic location, number, or alphanumeric location of a record within a conventional filing system.

alphabetic filing arrangement Records stored in dictionary order from A to Z by a person's name, business name, or subject name.

alphabetic index A listing of all names, subjects, or locations in a records filing system.

alphanumeric filing arrangement A combination of letters and numbers for storing records; similar to an outline.

aperture card A rectangular cutout card that holds one or more frames of microfilm.

application The third step in the life cycle of a record, describing the reason a record is created: to inform, make a decision, educate, collect statistics, etc.

archive record A record that is permanently preserved by an organization because of its historical value.

archives Storage location of records that are kept by an organization for a prolonged period of time.

ARMA (Association of Records Managers and Administrators) The leading professional organization in the records management and information fields, offering training and research opportunities.

as-written order The alphabetic indexing order by which business, government, and other names are filed.

bar coding Microfilm indexing method that introduces a pattern of clear and opaque bars between the images on film; similar to the bar codes on food and clothing.

blip coding Microfilm indexing method that makes a blip or mark next to each image and assigns each image a number.

block numeric coding A system in which the primary subjects are arranged alphabetically, with each subdivision given a block of numbers from the primary subject number.

centralized filing system Storage of all of the records of the organization in one location.

chargeout controls The tools used in *chargeout programs.*

chargeout log A written or electronic file indicating the name of the record, the borrower, the date of the loan, and the date the record is to be returned.

chargeout programs Guidelines for the loan and use of records.

chronological filing arrangement A system based on the date the record is needed rather than the information contained in the file folder; the three types of chronological filing arrangements are the pending file, the reading file, and the tickler file.

coding The physical activity of marking the filing units on a record to be stored.

color-coded filing system An arrangement that uses different colors to establish an indexing order with the use of tabs or folders.

compressor A moveable device at back of filing drawer that holds folders compact; also called a *follower block.*

computer-assisted retrieval (CAR) Technology that speeds retrieval of documents on microfilm through the use of the computer.

computer-based records system (CBRS) An automated records system that utilizes databases for the electronic storage and retrieval of information.

computer input microfilm (CIM) Technology that converts microfilm images to electronic signals on magnetic tape, which are then fed into the computer.

computer output to laser disk (COLD) The process of scanning paper documents to create electronic records saved on optical or magneto-optical disk.

computer output microfilm (COM) Technology that prints microforms from a computerized document file.

computer virus A program that infects computer files and programs, destroys information, and damages software.

consecutive numbering filing system Records arranged in ascending order, beginning with the lowest number and proceeding to the highest number; also called *sequential filing, serial numbering,* or *straight numeric filing.*

contact printing A method used for making duplicate copies of microforms.

creation The first step in the life cycle of a record, when data is recorded in a usable form manually or by a variety of means aided by technology.

cross-reference Documentation showing a secondary location where the record may be found.

database A collection of information that can be organized in a variety of ways to meet an organization's needs.

database management system (DBMS) A software program that integrates data files into databases that control and manipulate information.

data maintenance The addition, deletion, and reorganization of information by one user that

simultaneously preserves the accuracy of the information for other database users.

decentralized filing system Records stored throughout an organization in each individual department instead of one central location.

decimal filing A numeric arrangement based on the Dewey Decimal System, with nine main divisions (100-900) with nine subdivisions each, and a tenth division for categories too general for the nine main divisions.

density The measure of the amount of light that penetrates through the black areas of microforms.

dictionary arrangement The subject arrangement that stores records alphabetically from A to Z.

direct access database A system in which the computer goes directly to the location of the file requested.

direct access records system A system in which records are stored and retrieved directly without needing the assistance of an *index.*

directory A separate file in a database listing all of the information stored; also called an *index.*

disposition The final step in the life cycle of a record, describing what happens to the record once it has fulfilled its original purpose.

distribution The second step in the life cycle of a record, in which a document is physically or electronically delivered to its intended audience.

document An official business record.

duplex numeric filing A numeric filing system that uses numbers separated into two or more parts by a dash, period, space, or comma, with unlimited subdivisions of the main subject.

electronic document management system (EDMS) Technology that creates electronic images of paper records using electronic imaging or optical disk technology.

electronic file A mode of storage by computer.

Electronic Freedom of Information Act Amendment Legislation that grants public access to government documents through the federal government's Electronic Reading Room on the Internet.

electronic mail (e-mail) Messages sent automatically and electronically between computer users connected by a network.

electronic records system A system that stores records by using a computer and some type of disk media, involving database, word processing, and/or spreadsheet programs.

encyclopedic arrangement The subject storage arrangement that groups records by a main topic, with all related topics stored behind the main topic.

external documents Documents sent to individuals and companies doing business with the organization.

field A group of characters combined to create one unit of data.

file A collection of related records.

file manager A software application that controls the entry of the data and how it is organized in the database.

file name The title given each group of records following the protocol of the computer's operating system.

filing system The type of system used to store records; it describes the manner in which the records are organized.

fine sort An arrangement of all records in proper order before storing in the files; see also *rough sort*.

fiscal records The financial history of an organization.

flash cards or flash targets Cards that act as title pages identifying each batch of information or subject of microfilm/microfiche.

floppy disk A 3.5" external disk that provides secondary storage for a computer.

folder The storage container for individual records.

follower block A moveable device at back of filing drawer that holds folders compact; also called a compressor.

Freedom of Information Act (1966) Legislation that granted individuals the right to request information from federal agencies, except records that are protected from disclosure to the extent that the exemptions are contained in the law or in one of the three special law-enforcement record exclusions.

general record folder A container that holds miscellaneous records that do not have an individual folder; it is the last folder at the end of the corresponding letter of the alphabet.

geographic filing arrangement A system that stores records according to the location the record represents, instead of by name, number, or subject.

guide The divider used in all storage systems to separate each alphabetical letter, subject, location, or group of numbers.

hanging folder A folder with built-in hooks that allow it to hang from the parallel bars of the filing cabinet or a desk drawer; also called a *suspension folder*.

hard copy A paper document that may eventually be transferred to electronic form; also called a hard record.

hard disk The internally stored and permanently mounted disk in the computer.

historical records The history of an organization that may serve as a basis for future managerial decisions.

Hoover Commission (1946) An agency established by President Harry S. Truman to study the record-keeping needs of government agencies.

important records Records that are necessary for the operation of an organization.

inactive record A record kept in an off-site or on-site location that is not readily accessible but available when necessary.

index A separate file in a database listing all of the information stored; also called a *directory*.

indexing The mental process of determining the name of a record to be stored in the filing system; this is the most important step in the storage procedure.

indexing order The alphabetic order by which individual or personal names are filed.

indexing units The individual words and initials that make up the filing segment.

indirect access records system A system that requires an alphabetic index to store and retrieve records from the filing system.

inspecting The first step in the storage procedure; checking the record to make certain it has been released for filing.

internal documents Documents used only within an organization, and not distributed outside.

key field A field in a database with a unique value that permits records to be distinguished from one another; also called a *primary key*.

key unit The first unit of the filing segment.

label A surface on which to identify the contents of the file folder.

lateral filing cabinet Storage equipment available in letter and legal sizes and suited for long, narrow spaces because it is horizontally accessed.

legal records Records used for litigation purposes by an organization or retained by the organization for legal reasons.

life cycle of a record The stages a record goes through from the time it is created to the time it reaches its final resting place.

magnification ratio The measure of the relationship between the size of a microform image and the size of the document from which it was photographed; see also *reduction ratio*.

maintenance The fourth step in the life cycle of a record, involving the proper preservation of a record from its creation through its distribution and use.

manual records system The most basic method for filing documents; the organizing of records by hand using alphabetic, subject, geographic, and numeric filing arrangements.

master index Alphabetic list of all of the main topics in subject filing.

mechanical shelves Automated shelving in enclosed units with selector buttons for retrieval of records.

microfiche A sheet of 4 x 6" film, usually containing 96 reduced images to a card.

microfilm A continuous roll of 16mm or 33mm film designed to store reduced images of documents.

microfilm jacket Two sheets of acetate or plastic sealed at the top and bottom and divided into horizontal sections that hold strips of individual microfilm images cut from roll film.

microform The five types of micrographics: microfilm, microfilm jackets, microfiche, ultrafiche, and aperture cards.

micrographics records system Storage arrangement that reduces paper documents to miniature images on film; it is a cost-effective method for storing vast quantities of information in a limited amount of space.

middle-digit numeric filing A numeric filing arrangement for large volumes of records; a modification of the *terminal-digit numeric filing* arrangement.

nonessential records Records that are destroyed after they have served their purpose.

numeric filing arrangement Records stored by numbers instead of name, subject, or location; usually requires a corresponding *alphabetic index* to aid in storage and retrieval.

odometer indexing Micrographic indexing method that marks the distance of each image from the beginning of the roll of microfilm.

on-call form A record completed by a borrower when the file needed is already out on loan from the record center.

operating system Program that controls the operations of the computer; tells the applications how to perform their functions.

operational records Information vital to the daily operation of an organization.

open shelving The most economical type of filing equipment, in which records are stored horizontally on shelves instead of in enclosed cabinets; folders are arranged in rows, with tabs on the sides for easy reading and retrieval.

optical character recognition (OCR) Scanning of a document by light beams that first convert the document into an analog signal, and then into digital information that can be stored on optical disks.

optical disk Vehicle that stores information by burning the data onto the surface of the disk by using laser beams instead of magnetism.

out folder A folder that shows who borrowed the record and is placed in the file to replace the folder that has been borrowed.

out guide A guide placed in the location of the folder removed from the files; the borrower completes the loan information on the front of the out guide.

out indicator Identifies the record removed, who removed the record, and the date of the loan.

out slip A sheet of paper that is completed and filed in the folder when a single record or group of records are borrowed.

pending file A type of chronological filing arrangement that is a temporary checklist for items currently being processed; also called a suspense file.

periodic transfer method A system that designates specific time periods for the transfer of records from active to inactive storage.

perpetual transfer method A continual transfer process of records that occurs on a weekly, monthly, or bimonthly basis.

planetary camera A flatbed camera used for microfilming all types of documents.

primary guides The main divisions of the filing system (A, B, C, D, and so on).

primary key A field in a database with a unique value that permits records to be distinguished from one another; also called a *key field*.

Privacy Act (1974) Legislation that provided individuals with the ability to access information about themselves, the right to exclude others from obtaining information, and the right to know who has accessed their records.

Project ELF (Eliminate Legal-Size Files) A campaign by *ARMA* to standardize the documents in the judicial systems in America.

query A question asked of a database in order to solve a problem through retrieval of database information.

reader/printer A machine that displays an enlarged image of a microform onto a screen for viewing, with the added capability of printing a hard copy.

reader/viewer A machine that displays an enlarged image of a microform onto a screen for viewing.

reading file A chronological filing arrangement used by administrative personnel for easy access to copies of daily correspondence.

record A group of related fields containing information.

records center A centralized location in an organization that houses all records.

records inventory A physical accounting of the types, volume, and locations of a company's records; conducted before evaluating an existing retention schedule or developing a new one.

records management The systematic control of all records, from their creation or receipt, through processing, distribution, application, storage, and retrieval, to their final disposition.

records procedures manual A "how-to" reference book explaining a company's records system, procedures to be used in the records system, and the types of records stored.

records retention schedule A list of all records specifying the length of time records must be retained.

records transfer The moving of records from active to inactive storage.

records use analysis Part of a records inventory that helps identify how often files are actually used.

reduction ratio The measure of the relationship between the size of a document and the size of its microform image; see also *magnification ratio*.

reference document A document explaining how and why procedures are maintained by the organization, or containing information vital to the operation of the organization.

relative index An alphabetic list of the main topics, with every possible related topic, word, and word combination.

release mark The symbol used by an individual to show that he or she has finished using a document and it is ready to be stored in the filing system.

report generator The section of a database that searches and sorts the information requested by users from the database.

resolution The degree of sharpness of the film used for micrographics.

retrieval The process of locating and removing a record from the filing system.

reverse order The alphabetic order by which individual or personal names are filed.

rotary camera A micrographics camera with rotating belts that moves the documents through the machine as it advances the film; used for checks, invoices, and sales slips.

rough sort Records placed into an alphabetic or numeric sorter or folder behind the proper letter or number until the filer has time to sort and store the records; see also *fine sort*.

scores Ridges placed by the manufacturer along the base of the file folder to permit expansion.

scoring The process of manually creasing the ridges on the base of the folder; helps prevent overcrowding of the folder.

secondary guides Subdivisions of the *primary guides* (Ab, Ad, Al) for large filing systems.

sequential access database A system in which the computer reads through all files until it reaches the requested file.

sequential filing Records arranged in ascending order, beginning with lowest number and proceeding to the highest number; also called *consecutive numbering, serial numbering,* and *straight numeric filing.*

serial numbering Records arranged in ascending order, beginning with lowest number and proceeding to the highest number; also called *consecutive numbering, sequential filing,* and *straight numeric filing.*

soft copy Output seen on a computer screen or in microimages.

sorter A metal bar or folder with letters or numbers used for sorting records.

sorting Arranging records in the order in which they will be stored in the filing system.

step and repeat camera A micrographics camera used for microfiche, micropublishing books, catalogs, and parts and specification lists; it exposes images in rows and columns.

storing Placing the records in the filing system.

straight numeric filing Records arranged in ascending order, beginning with the lowest number and proceeding to the highest number; also called *consecutive numbering, sequential filing,* and *serial numbering.*

subject filing arrangement Records stored by the topic or subject contained in the record, instead of by the business or the individual's name.

suspense file A type of chronological filing arrangement that is a temporary checklist for items currently being processed; also called a *pending file.*

suspension folder A folder with built-in hooks that allow it to hang from the parallel bars of the filing cabinet or a desk drawer; also called a *hanging folder.*

tab A projection on the top edge or side of a folder or guide that extends above the regular height or width of the folder or guide; provides space for a label or caption.

terminal-digit numeric filing A numeric filing arrangement for large volumes of records, in which the numbers are divided into groups of twos and threes reading from right to left.

tickler file A type of chronological filing arrangement that serves as a reminder device for assignments or appointments due.

transaction documents Documents used to conduct the everyday operations of the organization.

ultrafiche The most extreme form of micrographics image reduction.

useful records Records used in the daily operation of an organization; if lost, they may cause delays or inconvenience, but will not damage a business.

vertical card file A cabinet that stores records upright in trays, drawers, or boxes, or in rotary and wheel files in card systems.

vertical filing cabinet The most commonly used storage equipment for alphabetic, subject, geographic, and numeric filing; uses the most aisle space.

visible card file Stores cards horizontally on flat trays, with the description of the card visible when the tray is open.

vital records Documents that answer the who, how, where, and when questions about an organization.

Answers

Answers to Memory File Questions

Chapter 1   Records Management: The Big Picture
True-False: 1 – T; 2 – F; 3 – F; 4 – F; 5 – F; 6 – F; 7 – T; 8 – T; 9 – T; 10 – T; 11 – T; 12 – F; 13 – T; 14 – T; 15 – T
Multiple Choice: 1 – a; 2 – c; 3 – b; 4 – d; 5 – c; 6 – b; 7 – c; 8 – d; 9 – c; 10 – b; 11 – d; 12 – b; 13 – c; 14 – a; 15 – b

Chapter 2   Records Management Systems
True-False: 1 – T; 2 – F; 3 – T; 4 – T; 5 – F; 6 – T; 7 – T; 8 – T; 9 – T; 10 – T; 11 – T; 12 – F; 13 – F; 14 – F; 15 – T
Multiple Choice: 1 – b; 2 – a; 3 – d; 4 – a; 5 – a; 6 – b; 7 – c; 8 – c; 9 – b; 10 – c; 11 – d; 12 – a; 13 – c; 14 – a; 15 – b

Chapter 3   Evaluating Manual Records Systems
True-False: 1 – T; 2 – T; 3 – T; 4 – T; 5 – T; 6 – T; 7 – F; 8 – T; 9 – T; 10 – F; 11 – T; 12 – T; 13 – T; 14 – F; 15 – T
Multiple Choice: 1 – d; 2 – c; 3 – d; 4 – b; 5 – c; 6 – a; 7 – d; 8 – c; 9 – d; 10 – c; 11 – c; 12 – b; 13 – c; 14 – a; 15 – d

Chapter 4   Manual Filing Systems
True-False: 1 – F; 2 – T; 3 – T; 4 – F; 5 – T; 6 – T; 7 – T; 8 – T; 9 – T; 10 – F; 11 – T; 12 – F; 13 – T; 14 – T; 15 – T
Multiple Choice: 1 – c; 2 – b; 3 – d; 4 – a; 5 – b; 6 – d; 7 – c; 8 – d; 9 – d; 10 – b; 11 – a; 12 – b; 13 – d; 14 – a; 15 – c

Chapter 5   Storage Solutions for Manual Records Systems
True-False: 1 – F; 2 – T; 3 – T; 4 – T; 5 – F; 6 – T; 7 – F; 8 – T; 9 – F; 10 – T; 11 – T; 12 – F; 13 – T; 14 – T; 15 – T
Multiple Choice: 1 – b; 2 – a; 3 – c; 4 – b; 5 – d; 6 – d; 7 – a; 8 – d; 9 – b; 10 – c; 11 – b; 12 – a; 13 – b; 14 – d; 15 – c

Chapter 6   Classifying Records for a Manual System
True-False: 1 – F; 2 – F; 3 – T; 4 – F; 5 – T; 6 – T; 7 – F; 8 – T; 9 – T; 10 – F; 11 - T; 12 – T; 13 – T; 14 – T; 15 – F
Multiple Choice:1 – b; 2 – b; 3 – a; 4 – c; 5 – c; 6 – b; 7 – d; 8 – d; 9 – d; 10 – a; 11 – c; 12 – b; 13 – b; 14 – c; 15 – b

Chapter 7   Subject and Geographic Filing Arrangements

True-False: 1 – T; 2 – F; 3 – T; 4 – F; 5 – T; 6 – T; 7 – T; 8 – T; 9 – F; 10 – F; 11 – T; 12 – T; 13 – T; 14 – T; 15 – F

Multiple Choice: 1 – c; 2 – d; 3 – b; 4 – a; 5 – c; 6 – a; 7 – b; 8 – c; 9 – c; 10 – c; 11 – c; 12 – a; 13 – d; 14 – a; 15 – c

Chapter 8   Numeric Filing Arrangements

True-False: 1 – F; 2 – F; 3 – T; 4 – T; 5 – F; 6 – F; 7 – T; 8 – T; 9 – F; 10 – T; 11 – T; 12 – T; 13 – T; 14 – T; 15 – T

Multiple Choice: 1 – b; 2 – b; 3 – a; 4 – d; 5 – d; 6 – a; 7 – c; 8 – d; 9 – d; 10 – a; 11 – d; 12 – a; 13 – b; 14 – c; 15 – b

Chapter 9   Micrographic Filing Systems

True-False: 1 – T; 2 – F; 3 – F; 4 – F; 5 – T; 6 – T; 7 – F; 8 – F; 9 – T; 10 – T; 11 – T; 12 – T; 13 – T; 14 – F; 15 – T

Multiple Choice: 1 – c; 2 – a; 3 – b; 4 – a; 5 – b; 6 – c; 7 – d; 8 – a; 9 – d; 10 – a; 11 – b; 12 – d; 13 – d; 14 – c; 15 – a

Chapter 10 Computer-Based Records Systems

True-False: 1 – T; 2 – T; 3 – T; 4 – F; 5 – F; 6 – T; 7 – T; 8 – T; 9 – T; 10 – F; 11 – F; 12 – F; 13 – T; 14 – T; 15 – F

Multiple Choice: 1 – a; 2 – b; 3 – a; 4 – d; 5 – b; 6 – c; 7 – d; 8 – d; 9 – b; 10 – c; 11 – c; 12 – b; 13 – d; 14 – d; 15 – d

Index

A

Abbreviations: business names, 121; personal names, 116

Access, 211; and equipment choices, 92; indirect, 142; from vertical cabinets, 94

Accession book, 165-166, 167, 177, 179

Accounting programs, 28

Accounting records, 102, 104, 107

Accounts payable invoices/bills, 104

Acronyms: in business names, 121

Active storage, 48, 54

Affiliates: alphabetizing, 126

Agents, 125, 126

Alphabetic card records, 72, 84

Alphabetic filing/filing arrangement, 3, 62, 84, 114-128; advantages/disadvantages with, 64; storage by subject within, 129

Alphabetic Filing Rules, 114

Alphabetic (or master) index, 65, 68, 107, 177; for alphanumeric filing, 173; for geographic filing, 152, 153, 155; for numeric filing, 164; for subject filing, 145, 149, 155. *See also* Indexes/Indexing

Alphabetic records arrangements: vertical cabinets for, 94

Alphanumeric filing/filing arrangements, 62, 84, 172-173; advantages/disadvantages with, 69; systems for, 179

Aperture cards, 191, 192, 201; storage for, 195

Apostrophes, personal names, 115

Application: of records, 24, 34

Appraisal: of records, 46

Arabic numerals, 164

Architectural drawings: and aperture cards, 191

Architectural records, 102, 105, 107

Archives, 54; file clerks in, 10; microfilm files in, 195; records in, 48

ARMA. *See* Association of Records Managers and Administrators

Articles: in business names, 120

Ascending numeric order, 122

Association names: alphabetizing, 124

Association of Records Managers and Administrators, 6, 7, 10, 13, 224; *Alphabetic Filing Rules*, 114; alphabetic filing rules for nonpersonal, nonbusiness names, 123-128

As-written order (straight order): business name captions in, 101; for filing, 75

Attributes: in relational database, 210

Audio clips, 211

Automated record systems, 208

B

Backlogging, 78

Backup disks, 214

Balance sheets, 104

Bar coding, 196, 201

Billing programs, 28

Blip coding, 196, 201

Block numeric filing systems, 174, 175, 179

Borough names: alphabetizing, 127, 128

Business names, 131; alphabetizing, 118-123; identical, 123; numbers in, 122; order of units, 119; prefixes, 120; prepositions, conjunctions, articles, and symbols, 120; punctuation and possessives, 120-121; single letters and abbreviations, 121; titles in, 121-122

C

Cabinet styles: lateral, 94-95, 107; mechanized, 95-96; open, 95; vertical, 93-94, 107

Calendar feature: in tickler file, 170

Call letters (radio and television): alphabetizing, 121

Cameras: for micrographics, 201

CAR. *See* Computer-assisted retrieval

Card cabinets: for microfiche, ultrafiche, aperture cards, 195

Card records, 107

Card systems, 102-103

Careers: in records management, 7, 8-11, 13. *See also* Records management in the real world

Cartridges: microfilm storage, 188

Case numbers: in legal offices, 65

Cassettes: microfilm storage, 188

CBRS. *See* Computer-based records systems

CD-R (Compact Disk-Recordable), 219

CD-ROM (Compact Disk-Read Only Memory), 27, 219, 226

CD-RW (Compact Disk-ReWritable), 219

CDs, 209, 213

Centralized filing systems, 24-25, 34

Certificates of authenticity: and scanned documents, 223

Certification: of records managers, 10

Certified Records Manager examination, 10

Chargeout procedures/programs, 25, 78-81, 84; controls, 49, 54; elements of, 79, 80; indicators, 79; log, 81; with numeric files, 175-176, 179

Charts: database creation of, 212, 226

Checkograph, 187

Checks, 104, 165

Chronological filing arrangements/systems, 62, 66-68, 84, 179; advantages/disadvantages with, 68; pending file, 170, 179; reading file, 170, 179; tickler or suspense file, 169-170, 179

CIM. *See* Computer input microfilm

City names: alphabetizing, 127, 128

Coding, 75, 84; for geographic filing arrangement, 151; of microforms, 196; of numeric records, 166; for subject filing, 142, 143

COLD. *See* Computer output to laser disk

Color-coded filing systems, 101-102, 130

COM. *See* Computer output microfilm

Commas: personal names, 115

Commonwealth names: alphabetizing, 127, 128

Company names. *See* Business names

Compressors, 93, 100

Computer-assisted retrieval, 198, 201

Computer-based records management (CBRM) programs, 211

Computer-based records systems, 207-232; description of, 208-209; storage in, 213-214

Computer input microfilm, 198, 201

Computer output microfilm, 198, 201

Computer output microfilm recorder, 193, 201

Computer output to laser disk, 221

Computers/computer technology, 3, 5, 31, 212-213; micrographics integrated with, 198, 201; and viruses, 29

Confidential information/records, 28, 176; chargeout procedures for, 79; control measures for, 49, 54; and numeric filing arrangements, 65, 175, 177. *See also* Chargeout procedures/programs; Security

Conjunctions: in business names, 120

Consecutive numbering filing systems, 164-166, 179

Contact printing: microforms, 197-198

Control procedures, 49, 54; for geographic filing arrangement, 152; for subject filing arrangement, 145. *See also* Chargeout procedures/programs

Correspondence: indexing tips for, 76

Correspondence folders: for geographic filing arrangement, 152; for subject filing arrangement, 144-145

Costs: and micrographics, 198-199, 224-225

County names: alphabetizing, 127, 128

Courier services, 23

Creation: of record, 23, 34

Cross-referencing, 77, 84; in geographic filing arrangement, 151, 152; of guardian/agent names, 125; of married woman's names, 117; in master index listing, 145; for numeric files, 175; for subject files, 142, 143; of unusual names, 115

Cuts: for tabs, 98

D

Dagron, Rene, 187

Dancer, John Benjamin, 187

Data: electronic storage of, 27; maintenance of, 209; security of, 214

Database management: software, 211; types of, 211

Database management system, 209

Database programs, 27, 211

Databases, 24, 208-209, 226; advantage/disadvantages with, 215; communication between computers and, 212-213; hierarchical, 210; network, 210; object-oriented, 211; organization of, 209-211; relational, 210

Database table: fields entered in, 209

dBase, 211

DBMS. *See* Database management system

Decentralized filing systems, 25, 34

Decimal filing systems, 172, 179

Density: microform developing, 197

Dewey, Melvil, 172

Dewey Decimal System, 103, 172

Dictionary arrangement, 69, 70, 155; for subject storage arrangement, 146-147

Dictionary order: in alphabetic filing, 63

Digital images, 219

Direct access database retrieval, 209

Directory: database, 212

Disk storage: computer-based records systems, 213

Disposal schedules: of numeric files, 175; for records, 43

Disposition: of records, 24, 34

Distribution: of records, 23, 34

Divisions: alphabetizing, 126; in geographic filing, 155

Documents, 3; classification of, by use or destination, 22; reducing to film, 196; release marks on, 143, 166; scanned, 220, 223. *See also* Files and filing; Records

Duplex numeric filing systems, 173, 174, 179

E

Electronic database management systems (EDMS): evaluating, 222

Electronic data storage, 27

Electronic decentralized filing system, 25

Electronic document management systems, 219, 226

Electronic files, 5, 7, 13

Electronic forms, 50; example of, 51

Electronic Freedom of Information Act, 6

Electronic imaging, 219, 226; advantages/disadvantages with, 221

Electronic Reading Room, 6

Electronic records systems, 8, 26-27, 28, 31, 34

Electronic storage, 62

Electronic systems: evaluation of, 222; legality of, 222-223

E-mail, 4, 30, 51, 226; address book feature, 217; file maintenance, 218; message, 217; Outlook e-mail client, 216; Select Names dialog box, 216, 217; storage folders, 218; using, 215; writing protocol, 217

Employee identification numbers, 177

Employee personnel records, 65

Encyclopedic arrangement, 69, 70, 155; file drawer organized in, 148; for subject storage arrangement, 147

Engineering drawings: and aperture cards, 191

Engineering records, 102, 105, 107

Enlarger-printer equipment, 194

Environmental controls: and computer-based records systems, 214

Equipment and supplies: for geographic filing arrangements, 151-152; for nonstandard records, 102-105, 107; for numeric filing arrangements, 176-177; photographic, for micrographics, 193; for records systems, 92-96, 107; retrieval/viewing, for micrographics, 193-194; for subject filing arrangements, 144-145

External audience, 22

External documents, 22

External records, 34

F

Fax machines, 4, 5, 23

Federal names: alphabetizing, 127

Federal Property and Administration Services Act, 5

Fields: within databases, 208, 209; in relational databases, 210; setting up, 213

Fifth-cut tabs, 98

Fifth position: of tab, 98

File clerks, 10

File manager: within database management system, 209

File names: database, 212

Files and filing, 7; alphabetic, 114-128; color-coded, 130; in databases, 208; electronic, 5, 7; hanging, 105; lost, 73, 76, 84; numeric, 163-184; and release marks, 74, 75; storage procedures for, 81; subject alphabetic, 129, 131. *See also* Manual filing arrangements/systems

Filing cabinets, 2; for geographic filing arrangements, 151, 155; for numeric filing arrangements, 176; for subject filing arrangements, 144, 155

Filing systems: centralized, 24-25, 34; color-coded, 101-102; decentralized, 25, 34; evolution of, 2; types of, 8, 13

Financial institutions: alphabetizing, 125; names of, 131

Financial statements, 104

Fine sort, 76

Fireproof cabinets, 94, 188, 214

First position: of tab, 98

Fiscal documents, 21, 31

Fiscal value, 34

Flash cards, 196, 201

Flash targets, 196, 201

Floor space, 93, 94

Floppy disks, 27, 31, 209, 213, 226

Folders, 96, 99-100; for decimal filing systems, 172; for geographic filing arrangements, 152; for numeric filing arrangements, 176; scoring, 107; for subject filing arrangements, 144. *See also* Files and filing

Follower block, 93, 100

Foreign article: in personal names, 114

Foreign government names: alphabetizing, 128, 129

Forms: database creation of, 212, 226; on-call, 79; reducing redundancy in, 50, 54

Fourth-cut tabs, 98

Franco-Prussian War, 187

Freedom of Information Act, 6

G

General record folders, 63-64

General Services Administration, 5

Geographic filing/filing arrangement, 62, 71, 84; advantages/disadvantages of, 72, 153; and alphabetic card indexes, 72; description of, 149-151; equipment/supplies for, 151-152; index for, 152-153; steps for processing records for, 151; steps for storing records in, 155

Geographic location: determining, 151

Geographic records arrangements: vertical cabinets for, 94

Given names, 114

Government: and records management, 5-6, 13

Government names: alphabetizing, 126-127

GSA. *See* General Services Administration

Guardians, 125, 126

Guides, 96-97; for consecutive numeric filing systems, 165; for geographic filing arrangements, 152; for microfiche, ultrafiche, aperture cards, 195; for numeric filing arrangements, 176; for subject filing arrangements, 144

Guide to Record Retention Requirements, 5

H

Hanging files/folders, 95, 100, 105

Hard copy, 7, 30

Hard disks, 27, 209, 213, 226

Hard drives, 31

Hard record, 7

Hashing, 209

Hierarchical database, 210

Historical records, 20

Historical value, 34

Hoover Commission, 6

Horizontal mechanized shelves, 96

Hyphens: in personal names, 115

I

ICRM. *See* Institute of Certified Records Managers

Identical names, 118, 123

Image-count marking, 196

Image Supervisor: sample job description for, 11

Important records, 21; keeping tabs on, 49

Inactive storage, 48, 54

Index (or reverse order): for personal names, 101, 114, 131

Indexes/indexing, 75, 84; alphabetic, 65, 68; alphabetic card, 72; of correspondence, 76; database, 212; for encyclopedic arrangements, 147; for geographic filing arrangements, 151, 152-153; of microforms, 196; and micrographics, 201; of numeric records, 166; odometer, 196, 201; for subject filing, 142, 143, 145-146; for terminal- and middle-digit filing systems, 168. *See also* Cross-referencing; Retrieval

Indirect access storage system, 142

Information: government handling of, 5

Information Age, 3, 4, 13

Information Society, 3

Information superhighway, 215

Information technology, 28

In-house database management programs, 211

Inspection: for geographic filing arrangement, 151; of numeric records, 166; of records, 74, 84, 142, 143

Institute of Certified Records Managers, 10, 13

Internal audience, 22

Internal documents, 22

Internal records, 34

Internal Revenue Service, 2, 21

International records: in geographic arrangement, 149, 150

Internet, 30, 215; Electronic Reading Room on, 6

Inventory: records, 46-48

Invoices, 65, 165

IT. *See* Information technology

J

Job descriptions: for Image Records Supervisor, 11; for Senior Records Clerk, Active Records, 11

Job opportunities: in records management, 9

Judicial Conference of the United States, 6

K

Key field: in database, 212

Key unit, 75

L

Labels/labeling, 75, 96, 100-101, 107; database creation of, 212, 226; for geographic filing arrangements, 152; for numeric filing arrangements, 176; for subject filing arrangements, 145; typing rules for, 101. *See also* Files and filing; Folders

Lateral cabinets, 94-95, 107; for geographic filing arrangements, 151, 155; for numeric filing arrangements, 176; for subject filing arrangements, 144

Law: and electronic systems, 222-223; and micrographics, 199, 201, 226; and records inventory, 46

Legal documents, 31

Legal records, 21, 102, 104-105, 107

Legal value, 34

Legislation: records management, 6

Letters, single: business names, 121

Library of Congress: microfilms at, 188

Library of Congress System, 103

License numbers, 164

M

Magnetic tapes, 27, 31, 214

Magnification ratio: in microform development, 197

Maintenance: of records, 24, 34

Manual filing arrangements/systems, 13, 61-90; alphabetic, 63-64; alphanumeric, 68; chronological, 66; color coding with, 102; geographic, 71; numeric, 65; subject, 69-70; types of, 62-71, 84

Manual filing systems tools, 96-101; folders, 96, 99-100; guides, 96-97; labels, 96, 100-101; tabs, 96, 97-98

Manual records systems, 8, 26, 31, 34; classification of records for, 113-139; evaluating, 41-60; storage solutions for, 91-112

Map cabinets, 105

Married women: personal names, 117-118

Master copy: microform, 197

Master index. *See* Alphabetic (or master) index

McCarthy, George, 187

Mechanical shelf filing: for numeric filing arrangements, 176

Mechanized shelves, 95-96, 107

Microfiche, 189-190, 201; storage of, 195

Microfilm, 187-189, 201; jacket, 189, 201; storage of, 195

Microform(s), 186; developing: terms, 197; indexing/coding during filming of, 196; reader-printer machine for, 194; resolution of, 197; types of, 187-191, 201

Micrographic filing systems, 13, 185-206; retrieval and viewing equipment for, 193-194

Micrographics, 29, 224-225; advantages/disadvantages of, 199; cost effectiveness of, 198-199; description of, 186; early tools in, 188; history of, 187; integration of, with computer technology, 198, 201; legality of, 199, 201, 226; as organizational solution, 192; and photographic equipment, 193; and records systems, 8, 31, 34

Micrographics preparation: film duplication, 197-198; film processing/developing, 197; indexing/coding during filming, 196

Microphotography, 187

Microsoft, 212

Middle-digit drawer, 169

Middle-digit filing systems, 167-169, 179

Military titles: in personal names, 116

Misfiling, 73, 76, 84

MO (magneto-optical) disk, 219

Motor vehicle departments, 164

MS-DOS, 212

N

Names, 114-118; county, 127, 128; federal, 127; given, 114; nicknames, 116; religious titles, 117; royal, 117; state, 127, 128; surnames, 114; trustee, 125, 126; unusual, 115; village, 127, 128. *See also* Business names; Personal names

National Archives and Records Administration (NARA), 5, 6

Network database, 210

Networked imaging systems, 221

Newspapers, 126

Nicknames, 116

Nonessential records, 22

Nonstandard records: equipment for, 102-105, 107

Numbers: in business names, 122

Numeric filing/filing arrangements, 62, 65, 72, 73, 84, 163-184; advantages/disadvantages with, 66, 175; alphabetic index with, 177; alphanumeric, 172-173; block numeric, 174, 175; chronological, 164, 169-171; consecutive number, 164; conversion elements for, 167; decimal, 172; duplex numeric, 173, 174; middle-digit, 164, 167-169; steps for storing records in, 179; terminal-digit, 164, 167-168; types of, 164-175, 179

Numeric records: steps for storing, 166; vertical cabinets for, 94

O

Object-oriented database, 211

OCR. *See* Optical character recognition

Odometer indexing, 196, 201

Off-site storage facilities, 10, 48

On-call form, 79

Open shelving filing systems, 95, 107, 176

Operating system: computer, 212

Operational records, 20-21

Operational value, 34

Optical character recognition, 219-220

Optical disks, 27, 31, 221; technology, 219, 224-225; types of, 219

Optical disk storage: equipment and process for, 219-221

Order of units: business or company names, 119; personal names, 114

Organization names: alphabetizing, 124

Organizing unit: in alphabetic manual filing system, 114

Out folder, 79, 80

Out guide, 79, 80

Out indicators, 78; for geographic filing arrangements, 152; in numeric files, 175; for subject filing arrangements, 145; types of, 79

Outlook (Microsoft): storage folders within e-mail program of, 218

Out slip, 79, 80

P

Paper records: and micrographics, 186

Paperwork: reducing, 50

Paperwork Reduction Act, 6

Paradox, 211

Parish names: alphabetizing, 127, 128

Particles: in personal names, 114

Pending file, 67, 68, 170, 171, 179

Periodicals, 126, 127

Periodic transfer method, 49

Periods: in personal names, 115

Perpetual transfer method, 48

Personal names, 131; abbreviations, 116; alphabetizing, 114-118; identical, 118; married women, 117-118; order of units, 114; prefixes, 114-115; punctuation, 115; religious and royal titles, 117; seniority, 116; titles and degrees, 116-117; unusual, 115

Personnel records, 177

Photocopiers, 4, 5

Photographic equipment: for micrographics records systems, 193

Photographs, 211

Pigeonhole shelves, 105

Planetary cameras, 193, 201

Position: of tab, 98

Possessives: in business names, 120-121

Postal deliveries, 23

Prefixes: in business names, 120; in personal names, 114

Prepositions: in business names, 120

Preprinted (or prenumbered) consecutive filing systems, 165

Primary guides, 63, 97

Primary key: in database, 212

Printers, 4, 5, 220

Printouts: computer-based records systems, 214

Privacy: and Internet, 6

Privacy Act, 6

Productivity, 4

Professional organizations: for records management, 6, 13

Project ELF (Eliminate Legal-Size Files), 104

Province names: alphabetizing, 127, 128

Publications/Published materials, 102, 103-104, 107, 126, 127

Punctuation: in business names, 120-121; in personal names, 115

Purchase orders, 65, 165

Q

Queries: database, 212-213, 226

Questionnaires: for assessing records system, 43

R

R:Base, 211

Reader-printer, 201

Reader-printer equipment, 194

Reader-viewer, 201

Reader-viewer equipment, 194

Reading file, 68, 170, 171, 179

Receivers, 125, 126

Record keeping: early examples of, 2

Records, 7, 34; classification of, 22, 113-139; coding, 75, 84; cross-referencing, 77, 84; within databases, 208; filing by subject, 142; indexing, 75; inspecting, 84; levels of usefulness, 21-22; life cycle of, 23-24, 34; lost, 73, 76, 84; nonessential, 22; numeric, 163-184; requests and chargeout procedures for, 78-81; sorting, 84; storing, 4, 24-25, 74-77, 84; transfer methods, 48-49; use analysis, 46, 54; value placed on, 20-21, 34. *See also* Documents; Files and filing; Folders

Records and information director, 9

Records and Information Management (RIM) department, 9

Records archive, 48

Records centers, 24; chargeout procedures in, 78-81

Records clerks, 9

Records inventory: keeping track with, 46-48

Records management: careers in, 7, 8-11; and computer technology, 208; defined, 7, 13; federal case of, 5-6; importance of, in workplace, 2; professional organizations for, 6, 13; specialized terms in, 7-8; systems, 19-40

Records management in the real world: accounting department, 178; career path at furniture manufacturer, 52-53; color-coded alphabetic filing system, 130; continuation folders, 106; geographic filing arrangement, 154; junior college, 32-33; micrographic filing systems, 200; micrographics/optical disk storage, 224-225; misfiled transcript tracking, 82-83; specialty clothing store, 12

Records management personnel: organizational chart for, 9

Records managers: certification for, 10

Records procedures manual, 47, 54

Records retention schedule, 54

Records survey, 43

Records systems, 20; advantages/disadvantages with, 29; assessing/improving, 42-44; control procedures for, 49; equipment for, 92-96, 107; integrating, 30-31. *See also* Cabinet styles

Reduction ratio: in microform developing, 197

Reels: microfilm storage, 188

Reference documents, 22, 34

Relations: in relational database, 210

Relative index: in alphanumeric filing, 173; for geographic filing arrangements, 155; for subject filing arrangements, 146, 149, 155

Release marks, 74, 75, 143, 166

Religious institution names, 124, 131

Religious titles: in personal names, 117

Report generator: within database management system, 209

Reports: database creation of, 212, 226

Requests: for records, 78

Resolution: microform, 197

Retention: disposition of records in, 45; periods, 45

Retention schedules, 42, 43, 44; of numeric files, 175; sample, 46

Retrieval, 142, 148; computer-assisted, microfilm, 198; database, 208, 209; from geographic filing arrangements, 153; of microform images, 186; from open shelving, 95; of scanned documents, 220; from subject alphabetical files, 129; from vertical cabinets, 94. *See also* Indexes/indexing

Reverse order filing, 75, 101, 114, 131

Ridges: of folder, 99

Roll film storage, 195

Rotary cameras, 193, 201

Rough sort, 76

Rows: in relational database, 210

Royal titles, 117

S

Scanners and scanning, 219, 220, 223

School names, 124, 131

Scores and scoring: on folders, 99, 100, 107

Secondary guides, 97

Security, 28; clearance, 25; codes, 24; data, 214; and equipment choices, 93; and micrographics, 199; and

numeric filing arrangements, 176, 177. *See also* Chargeout procedures/programs

Seniority designations: in personal names, 116

Senior Records Clerk, Active Records: sample job description for, 11

Sequential access database retrieval, 209

Sequential filing, 164, 179

Serial numbering, 164, 179

Shelving: mechanized, 107; open, 107

Shortened names, 116

Social security numbers, 164, 177

Soft copy, 7

Software, 208; database management, 211

Sorters, 102

Sorting, 76, 84; for geographic filing, 151; of numeric records, 166; for subject filing, 142, 144; tips, 64

Space: and micrographics, 198

Special guides: for subject filing arrangements, 144

Spreadsheet programs, 27

Staggered-line position: of tab, 98, 99

State names: alphabetizing, 127, 128

Step and repeat cameras, 193, 201

Storage, 81; active, 48, 54; in computer-based systems, 213-214; electronic, 62; for geographic filing arrangement, 151; inactive, 48, 54; for manual records systems, 91-112; and microfilm, 188; for micrographics systems, 195; of numeric records, 166; optical disk, 219-221; permanent, 45; for records, 24-25, 74-77, 84, 146-147; for subject filing, 142, 144; by subject within alphabetic arrangement, 129; tips, 74. *See also* Cabinet styles; Equipment and supplies

Straight-cut tabs, 98

Straight-line position: of tab, 98, 99

Straight numeric filing, 164, 179

Student identification numbers, 164

Subdivisions/Subdivision guides: for geographic filing arrangement, 152, 155

Subject alphabetic filing, 131

Subject alphabetic arrangement: storage by, 129

Subject filing/filing arrangements, 62, 69-70, 84; advantages/disadvantages of, 71, 148-149; and alphabetic card indexes, 72, 73; description of, 142; equipment/supplies for, 144-145; indexes for, 145-146; steps for processing records for, 142-144; steps for storing records in, 155

Subject records arrangements: vertical cabinets for, 94

Subject storage arrangements: types of, 146-147, 155

Subject title: determining, 143

Subsidiaries: alphabetizing, 126

Surnames, 114
Suspense files, 68, 95, 169-170, 179
Suspension folders, 100
Symbols: in business names, 120
System analysis team, 42, 43, 44

T

Tables: database creation of, 212, 226; in relational
  databases, 210
Tabs, 96, 97-98. *See also* Guides
Tape cartridge, 27
Tape reel, 27
Tax information, 21, 104
Technology, 4
Telecommunications, 30
Terminal-digit drawer, 168
Terminal-digit filing systems, 167-168, 179
Territory names: alphabetizing, 127, 128
Third-cut tabs, 98
Tickler file, 67, 169-170, 171, 179
Titles/degrees: in business names, 121-122; in personal
  names, 116-117
Town/township names: alphabetizing, 127, 128
Training: about encyclopedic arrangements, 147; and
  micrographics, 199
Transaction documents, 22, 34
Truman, Harry, 6
Trustee names, 125, 126
Tuples: in relational database, 210
Turnaround time, 47

U

Ultrafiche, 191, 201; storage of, 195
Uniform Photographic Copies of Business and Public
  Records as Evidence Act of 1951, 199, 201, 222
Units: of filing segment, 75; identifying, 75
Unusual names: alphabetizing, 115
Useful records, 22

V

Vertical card file, 102-103
Vertical filing cabinets, 93-94, 107; for geographic fil-
  ing arrangements, 151; for numeric filing arrange-
  ments, 176; for subject filing arrangements, 144, 155
Video, 211
Village names: alphabetizing, 127, 128
Virus: computer, 29
Visible card file, 103
Vital records, 21
Vouchers, 65, 104, 165

W

Windows 95, 98, 2000 (Microsoft), 212
Word processing, 4, 27
Working copy: microform, 197
World War II: micrographics used during, 187

Y

Yellow Pages, 142